Experiencing the Intimacy
of Jesus' Touch

An
Undivided
Heart

Rita J. Platt

NAVPRESS⬤

NavPress is the publishing ministry of The Navigators, an international Christian organization and leader in personal spiritual development. NavPress is committed to helping people grow spiritually and enjoy lives of meaning and hope through personal and group resources that are biblically rooted, culturally relevant, and highly practical.

For a free catalog go to www.NavPress.com
or call 1.800.366.7788 in the United States or 1.800.839.4769 in Canada.

ISBN-13: 978-1-60006-388-6

Cover design by Arvid Wallen
Cover image by Shutterstock

Some of the anecdotal illustrations in this book are true to life and are included with the permission of the persons involved. All other illustrations are composites of real situations, and any resemblance to people living or dead is coincidental.

Printed in the United States of America

1 2 3 4 5 6 7 8 / 13 12 11 10 09

For Mom,

who flew to my side when my heart was breaking.

You bless me by sharing in the laughter and the tears.

Also by Rita J. Platt:

I Am His

Step into the Waters

Contents

Acknowledgments

Thom, you sacrificed over and over that I might have the privilege of pursuing my dreams. I hope for many more years to dream together.

I'm forever indebted to the women who opened their hearts to me. Your desire to know the wonder of relationship, to experience connection, not just follow a religion, was inspiring. Through your longing, you helped me dream of eternal romance and ultimate wholeness. Thank you for sharing.

During the writing of this study, I was gifted with new friendship. Chuck and Carol McIlHenny, Jim and Marilyn Harrington, Wayne and Deb Wheeler, Mark and Jill Sotosky, please know how glad I am that the Lord placed you in my path. You quickly took me into your hearts and demonstrated true community and fellowship.

I have the best brothers a girl could have. Neil and Doyle, I don't know how to thank you. Though we've each embraced different challenges, we face them together. I love you guys.

I could not have moved forward with this study without the prayers of cherished friends. Chris Sabin, Susan Hamel, Deb French, Sharon Hagar, Ann Norton, Debbie Mendoza, and Pam Grace, I'm so grateful you took the time to lift me to the Lord.

I've been graced by the kindness of my editor, Rebekah Guzman, and the NavPress team. Thank you for your understanding when I walked through difficult times. I feel privileged to work with a group dedicated to making love known in words and actions.

And above all, thank you to the Lord Jesus. There are no words that express what it means to me to know You. Continue to capture every piece of my heart.

To Know Him Is to Love Him

Do you believe in love at first sight? Some couples adamantly proclaim they knew they would marry the moment they met. Others think that is unlikely, that lasting love takes much more time to develop. Most, however, would agree that it's wonderful when love deepens and matures the more a couple gets to know one another.

A few months ago, I had the opportunity to hear a few real-life love stories. My husband and I were having dinner with new acquaintances. Somehow the conversation meandered toward stories of how each couple met and eventually married. Each story was unique, and some of the details were a complete surprise.

Recall your favorite love story. Maybe it's a true story or one you've seen in a movie. What is it about that story that touches your heart?

Have you ever thought of the Bible as an epic love story? It's filled with passion and heart-stopping moments that change lives for all eternity. Psalm 107 tells stories of the struggle to survive apart from the Lord. In each scenario, the Lord ultimately provides redemption. The psalm culminates with these words in verse 43: "Whoever is wise, let him heed these things and consider the great love of the LORD."

Jesus beckons us to respond to His immense love. He said, "Greater love has no one than this, that he lay down his life for his friends" (John 15:13). He's freely opened His heart to us, laying down His life to invite us to know Him intimately. He doesn't offer anything but the best. His love is more than a gushy sentiment: It's solid, unconditional, and eternal. Jesus' love pursues and summons us simultaneously. It calls us to open every chamber of our hearts to His touch.

How did your love story with Jesus begin? Where did you first meet Him? Spend a few moments recalling and jotting down the circumstances surrounding the initial moments that launched your personal relationship with Jesus.

If you have not yet begun that love story, please consider this a personal invitation to an eternal romance that will never fade. Jesus extends Himself for you and to you in the most loving way possible. No shame, no wrong is too great for His love to overcome. He surrendered His life on the cross to pay for your every sin, and He rose from the dead so that through Him you too can live. You can respond to His love by praying,

Lord Jesus, I know I have sinned and need the
forgiveness and life You offer. I believe that You died

to pay for my sin and that You rose from the dead.
I turn to You; I hand over my life to You. Please
forgive me and grant me a heart that desires to walk
with You above all else. Thank You for making
me clean and for blessing me with the privilege of
belonging to You forever. Amen.

If you prayed this prayer today for the first time, my heart rejoices with you. No matter what life may throw your way, from this point on, you'll never be alone. You belong to the Lord Jesus Christ, and you've begun a journey into a love so deep that it will take an eternity to explore.

Whether you've just met Jesus for the first time or you've known Him for years, He loves you unconditionally. As you journey with your hand in His, He leads your heart to completeness in Him. He knows exactly where you are today, what challenges you're facing, and how best to bring wholeness to your life. Reflect for a minute on your personal journey. What type of symbol would you use to describe your heart today?

- Waters that seem tranquil until stirred up
- A puzzle with a few pieces missing or out of place
- Two people running toward one another through a field of flowers in slow motion
- A clouded mirror
- A scuba diver exploring the depths of the sea
- A thirsty runner panting for a break
- Other _____

Pause for a moment to lay your heart just as it is before Jesus. Tell Him about your hopes and desires as you begin this study. Ask Him to meet you where you are now and capture every inch of your heart, filling it with His love.

Ponder Scripture

So long as we imagine it is we who have to look for God, we must often lose heart. But it is the other way about—He is looking for us.

—Simon Tugwell

Jesus came in pursuit of your whole heart. He didn't wait for you to come looking for Him. He wants you to belong to Him, to give your hand to Him, to embark on an eternal love relationship. He paid an exquisite price to make that happen.

Meditate on the following verses from *The Message*:

> Christ arrives right on time to make this happen. He didn't, and doesn't, wait for us to get ready. He presented himself for this sacrificial death when we were far too weak and rebellious to do anything to get ourselves ready. (Romans 5:6)

> He used his servant body to carry our sins to the Cross so we could be rid of sin, free to live the right way. His wounds became your healing. You were lost sheep with no idea who you were or where you were going. Now you're named and kept for good by the Shepherd of your souls. (1 Peter 2:24-25)

Silently dwell on the demonstration of Jesus' love. How does it feel to be pursued with such intensity?

Jesus endured horrific anguish of body and soul to gift us with a love beyond our wildest dreams, a red-hot love that invites us to respond with our entire being. He doesn't look at you or me and say, "She's too damaged, soiled, unknown, wealthy, poor, and unattractive to love." He knows everything there is to know about you—every detail, all the pleasing and putrid moments of your life—and still pursues you with a passion you can barely imagine.

The more I walk with Jesus, the more His call to life, to wholeness for His beloved, resounds in my soul. I hear His desire to open closed rooms, clear out the cobwebs, and bring fresh air and the fragrance of His love. He wants to draw us deeper into His embrace, to free us to live undivided.

Will you please pray with me?

> *Dear Lord Jesus, I'm so grateful for Your persistent pursuit. You know me through and through. You know the open places in my heart and the places I'm reluctant to expose. Please bathe every nook and cranny in Your love. The more I know You, Lord, the more I love You. Take me deeper, Lord. Reveal Yourself to me; remind me of Your majesty and Your goodness. Teach me to trust You wholeheartedly. Cause me to fall head over heels in love with You all over again. Amen.*

The Name of Jesus

When we meet someone new, one of the first things we do is exchange names. It is rare to learn much from a name today other than how to address someone. However, occasionally a name gives us extra insight. For example, the name Nevaeh, one I'd not heard until a few years ago, has been cropping up more and more. When I comment on the name, parents share that it is *heaven* spelled backward. Sometimes they elaborate even further, explaining the circumstances surrounding their baby's birth. They describe feeling upended and overwhelmed by their pregnancy at first but eventually embracing this new life within and welcoming their baby as a precious gift from heaven. Hearing their stories lends new significance to the name.

In the Bible, names carry deep meaning. They reveal the character of a person. Jesus' name offers so much more than an arrangement of letters we put together so we know what to call Him. His name opens the door to experiential knowing, to an intimacy that seeps into the cracks of our hearts.

Experiencing Jesus' Name

I sat by myself on the edge of a chair just outside a hospital procedure room. My husband was undergoing a routine test that turned into an event rivaling the impact of a sudden hurricane. During the "routine" procedure, his lung collapsed. Eyes wide and heart racing, I stayed anchored to my chair. The activity of frantic medical personnel mixed with the crashing sounds of pain swirled around me. My panicked heart threatened to collapse into fragmented debris, when the voice of the Lord stilled my spirit. He said, "Rita, whatever happens, whether Thom lives or dies, you will be okay because I am here." I know I may have looked all alone sitting on that chair, but I was not alone. I knew that God was with me, and that experiential knowing changed everything. He was and is my Immanuel (which means "God with us").

Celebrate with me the words of Isaiah 9:6-7 by proclaiming them aloud and pausing to enjoy each name:

His names will be: Amazing Counselor,
    Strong God,
Eternal Father,
    Prince of Wholeness.
His ruling authority will grow,
    and there'll be no limits to the wholeness he brings. (MSG)

Please look up the following verses and take note of the names given to Jesus.

- ◆ Luke 1:31 _____
- ◆ Luke 2:11 _____
- ◆ John 1:29 _____
- ◆ 1 Corinthians 10:4 _____
- ◆ Revelation 1:8 _____
- ◆ Revelation 19:16 _____

Which of Jesus' names do you most sense a need to know today? Journal your need and ask Jesus to take you to deeper intimacy through His name.

A Few Revealing Encounters

It's often enlightening to observe interactions of people. Immerse yourself in each of the following passages, picturing the details and jotting down key words or phrases that reveal Jesus' character. Then imagine you are filming each scene. What expression would be on the face of each character? What intonation of voices do you hear?

- ◆   Matthew 19:13-15

♦   Luke 7:11-17

♦   John 13:1-17

Glance back over your notes. What do you think Jesus is saying to you today about who He is?

What action can you take based on how He's revealing Himself to you?

Show Me

In the musical *My Fair Lady*, Eliza is eating and breathing speech exercises. At the same time, Freddy ardently pursues her with words until she becomes exasperated and sings, in the song "Show Me," about needing to see actions. Have you ever been in the place where you can't quite absorb the truth of words and wish for some action that makes Jesus' heart known? I've been in that place.

I was preparing to move across the country to somewhere I'd never even visited and was struggling with apprehension. I knew in my head that Jesus was there and directing this move, but my heart was having trouble absorbing His assurance. In the midst of dealing with the unending details of moving, the doorbell rang. When I opened the door, I was greeted with a beautiful bouquet of flowers. Later I learned that a friend had been awakened in the middle of the night with the Lord impressing this thought on her heart: "Send Rita flowers." What a sweet demonstration of love. Jesus had my friend send me flowers to reassure me of His abiding presence in the midst of trying days. Then He pointed me to a Scripture passage that reminded me that wherever I go, He will always be there ahead of me and hold me fast (see Psalm 139:7-10).

John the Baptist, a man of incredible faith, also had a moment when he needed some reassurance. Please read Luke 7:18-23. What actions did Jesus highlight to reassure John?

In what area's of life are you needing the reassurance of who Jesus is and His involvement in your life?

Pray through Psalm 86 aloud with those areas in mind, and then spend a few moments sitting quietly and journaling any thoughts. Conclude that time by proclaiming the words of the wonderful old hymn "No One Ever Cared for Me Like Jesus." If you know the melody, try singing it; otherwise, simply say the words and let them speak to your heart.

> No one ever cared for me like Jesus
> There's no other friend so kind as he
> No one else could take the sin and darkness from me
> Oh how much he cares for me.[1]

Reflect

Have you ever wondered about the meaning of a candle and what it stands for? The use of candles can be traced to the night of Passover, the Lord's Easter. The early Christians used candles to symbolize Christ's presence amidst the darkness of the world. Just as Christ is the light of the world and has consummated himself for love, the candle offers its light by consummating itself.

— CARLO CARRETTO, *GOD'S NAME IS LOVE*

Consider arranging an intimate candlelight dinner with Jesus. Put flowers on the table, use a special tablecloth, eat from your best dishes, or do whatever you can to set the stage. If you don't like to cook, maybe you could buy an already-prepared meal or get takeout from your favorite restaurant. As you light the candles, keep in mind the meaning of the candle. Imagine that Jesus is sitting in the chair next to you.

How will you tell Him you love Him? What do you see in His eyes? What do you want to know about Him?

Try pouring out your love by reading the following prayer of John of the Cross and then adding your own words:

O Living Flame of Love . . .
How Gently and how lovingly
Thou wakest in my bosom,
Where alone thou secretly dwellest;
And in Thy sweet breathing
Full of grace and glory,
How tenderly Thou fillest me with Thy love.[2]

Respond

Take in the words of Luke 7:36-38. Pretend that like the woman in this passage you are pouring out your gratitude and worship at the feet of Jesus. If you can, find your favorite perfume or scent and breathe it in as you kneel before Him. Picture yourself pouring out a love as wonderful as that scent. As you rise, do so asking Him to bless you with knowledge of Him that can't help but become an ever-deepening love. Let the fragrance of this moment surround you throughout the week by keeping your chosen scent in a place you'll be aware of it regularly. End this time with the following old Irish prayer:

I beseech you, Jesus, loving Saviour, to show yourself to all who seek you so that we may know you and love you. May we love you alone, desire you alone, and keep you always in our thoughts. May love for you possess our hearts. May affection for you fill our sense, so that we may love all else in you. Jesus, King of Glory, you know how to give greatly. And you have promised great things. Nothing is greater than yourself. We ask nothing else of you but yourself. You are our life, our light, our food and our drink, our God and our all.[3]

Complete Freedom

Deliver me from me and deliver me to you.

— MARGARET BECKER

Answering health history questions in the doctor's office brought a flush of shame to my face. The doctor asked me how many times I've been pregnant and the ages of my children. I hung my head and hesitated like a criminal. Most people quickly identify me as the mother of three sons. The truth includes more information. At fifteen years old, I was pregnant and placed a baby girl up for adoption. I wanted to be honest with the doctor but didn't want to explain what I saw as my failure. I carried secret shame around like a second skin. It's only been through knowing Jesus that I have been able to shed the shame and experience complete freedom from my past.

Here or in your journal, note any regret, shame, fear, secret grief, negative attitude, destructive self-talk, or failure that haunts you.

Maybe you aren't constricted by your past but stand, as we all do, in need of continual grace to walk free from sin into the future. Name any struggles that seem to resurface.

Galatians 5:1 says, "It is for freedom that Christ has set us free. Stand firm, then, and do not let yourselves be burdened again by a yoke of slavery." What would it look like to live completely free?

Speak to Jesus of your hopes and fears about looking to Him alone for complete deliverance.

Ponder Scripture

The television series *Heroes* and superhero movies like *Spider-Man*, *Batman*, and *Iron Man* are increasing in popularity. An old pop song laments, "I'm holding out for a hero 'til the end of the night."[1] Chains that threaten to strangle us seem too powerful for mere humans to break. Have you found yourself wishing for a hero to suddenly ride in and rescue your heart?

The woman who reached to touch Jesus' robe knew that sense of need. In her desperation, she extended her fingers hoping for supernatural help, but she needed someone real, someone more than a legendary character composed of wishful thinking. She needed real connection with Jesus, physical touch that became more than physical.

Please read Mark 5:25-34 and Luke 8:43-48. We aren't given many details about this woman's life, but we do know that women who were bleeding were considered unclean. Their status was contagious. Anyone who touched them also became unclean. "It is probable that the woman with an issue of blood . . . had menorrhagia, a disease in which the menstrual flow is abnormally prolonged—in her case continuous for 12 years—and may produce anemia."[2] Even during the normal time of menstruation, women were rendered unclean (see Leviticus 15:33). This was no fleeting feeling of embarrassment; for twelve long years, she endured chronic suffering.

What words or phrases would you use to describe how it feels to live with ongoing pain or shame?

Read Mark 5:25-34 and Luke 8:43-48 one more time and add details to the following table from each passage:

Setting	
Main Characters	
Secondary Characters	
Pivotal Moments	

Because others avoided contamination or becoming unclean, I wonder how often this woman was actually touched, if at all. Did she crave physical contact or hunger for a hug? Did anyone ever accidentally brush up against her? My heart aches for her when I consider the need we all share to experience physical contact.

When my twin sons were born three months early, I witnessed firsthand the power of human touch. Their little bodies were invaded by ominous-looking wires and tubes, but I was given permission to reach in and stroke their heads and hold their tiny hands. My heart longed to touch their hearts. Skin met skin, and I believe that somehow in those moments, we bonded. The significance of that connection was stressed when I heard about babies languishing—some even dying—in part because there was no one to touch or hold them. How amazing that a simple touch creates an atmosphere in which we can flourish and affirms that we're alive, creating freedom to love and be loved.

What desperation the woman must have felt as she did the unthinkable: reached out and touched Jesus. Even though the woman received the healing she sought, Mark 5:33 says that she "came and fell at his feet and, trembling with fear, told him the whole truth." If you were this woman, what would have been your deepest fear?

Pause for a moment, close your eyes, and imagine you are the woman with the bleeding issue. Choose one or more of the following exercises to explore:

- Write a brief journal entry describing the woman's encounter with Jesus from her perspective.
- Describe a time when you felt desperate for connection, physical or otherwise.

◆ How many times this brave woman must have worked to slip in and out of an area unobtrusively. How would it feel to live like this? In what sense do you try to hide pieces of yourself? What prompts the instinct to hide?

Luke 8:43 points out that the woman was subject to her condition. Her bleeding had control over her life. It dictated daily movements. Because of it, she could not live freely. At times, we too live subjected to a condition that divides our hearts, becoming enslaved to something or someone other than Jesus. As you read the stories that follow, notice and name the chains that keep each woman bound.

Beth's Story

Shame can be described as "a paralyzing emotion in which the afflicted person believes irreparable damage has been done to the deepest part of her soul. . . . Sufferers describe this feeling as an internal wound so painful and heavy that it makes them feel flawed for even existing."[3] Beth knew shame intimately. She told a story that still filled her eyes with tears years later. As a young woman, Beth made a choice to have an abortion. Now when she talks about the details, it's as though the pain is still being wrung as from a wet cloth dripping with self-recriminations, regret, and if-onlys. Beth tried for years to punish herself and, at the same, justify her actions. She lived under a cloud of shame, divided even from herself. She felt as if she could never be truly whole again in the Lord's presence.

Linnette's Story

"False, or unhealthy, guilt arises from listening to the condemning voice of the Pharisee within. It's caused by heeding the lie that says we gain God's favor by living up to the bar of absolute perfection."[4] False guilt may also originate from exposure to legalistic religiosity or other sources. Linnette dragged a tired sense of defeat wherever she went. Shoulds and oughts plagued her. They bounced around her mind persistently. She spent enormous amounts of energy analyzing each one and using it as a measuring stick for her every thought, attitude, and action. She felt she should never be angry, should not voice her opinion, ought to always have a clean house when guests arrived, should never consider her own needs, should never be out sick from work, and the list went on. Relentlessly, Linnette policed herself, thinking she'd never be a good-enough Christian.

Miranda's Story

Miranda knew what it meant to have someone she should have been able to trust rip her heart to shreds. She asked, *What makes my mother hurt me?* She feared her mom, never knowing at what moment she would lash out, yet craved her love. Miranda harbored a core belief that she must be defective. Shame scented her daily relationships and began seeping into any hope for a better future. "Physical and sexual abuse are both illegal. Although there are no laws against verbal violence, it remains an active and destructive form of abuse. Raging shrieks leave bruises that will never be seen but are painfully felt."[5]

My Story

Before I became a Christ follower, I initiated a divorce and remarried not long afterward. My children were quite young, yet they were hurt deeply by my actions. Guilt became my silent companion. When I met Jesus, I was overwhelmed by His love and forgiveness. Still, guilt hadn't moved out of my heart. Whenever I was asked a simple question like "How many children do you and your husband have?" I felt compelled to apologize for my behavior and divorce over and over again in word and deed. It was as if there were segments of myself that were somewhat presentable in Christian circles and those that were not. My very real guilt was covered by the blood of Jesus, but I hung on to the guilt, living under its shadow. I could not forgive myself. I lived with the illusion that I was the "final judge."[6]

Do any of the above-mentioned stories strike a chord with you. If so, in what ways? If not, is there any other sense in which your heart is subject to something or someone other than Jesus?

Let's return once more to the story of the woman with the issue of blood and read it aloud in Mark 5:25-34, this time from *The Message*:

A woman who had suffered a condition of hemorrhaging for twelve years—a long succession of physicians had treated her, and treated her badly, taking all her money and leaving her worse off than before—had heard about Jesus. She slipped in from behind and touched his robe. She was thinking to herself, "If I can put a finger on his robe, I can get well." The moment she did it, the flow of blood dried up. She could feel the change and knew her plague was over and done with.

At the same moment, Jesus felt energy discharging from him. He turned around to the crowd and asked, "Who touched my robe?"

His disciples said, "What are you talking about? With this crowd pushing and jostling you, you're asking, 'Who touched me?' Dozens have touched you!"

But he went on asking, looking around to see who had done it. The woman, knowing what had happened, knowing she was the one, stepped up in fear and trembling, knelt before him, and gave him the whole story.

Jesus said to her, "Daughter, you took a risk of faith, and now you're healed and whole. Live well, live blessed! Be healed of your plague."

Whatever your source of bleeding pain, Jesus is near, ready to receive and heal your brokenness. Only in Jesus can your fragmented heart become whole; only in Jesus can you be completely free. He is the one true Deliverer. Will you take a risk of faith and reach for grace? Will you come to His feet and spill the complete story of your need? What is the size and shape of your struggle? Where did it begin? Fill in this table with the details of your personal story.

Setting	
Main Characters	
Secondary Characters	
Main Events	
Evidence of Destruction	

Will you consider inviting Jesus to intervene and make today a pivotal moment in your story? He sees you. He looks past the externals to the depths pooled behind your eyes and really sees you. He aches to pour out deliverance. His love is a synergy of tenderness and power; it's life-altering. Go back through the table you filled in and ask Jesus to touch each detail with life and freedom. If you are able, kneel where you are and wait in silence for a few minutes.

Hear Jesus speak to you: "Daughter, your faith has healed you. Go in peace and be freed from your suffering" (Mark 5:34). Read it aloud emphasizing different words each time as follows:

Daughter, your faith has healed you. Go in peace and be freed
from your suffering.

Daughter, your faith has **healed you**. Go in peace and be freed
from your suffering.

Daughter, your faith has healed you. **Go in peace** and be freed
from your suffering.

Daughter, your faith has healed you. Go in peace and **be freed**
from your suffering.

If you wish, pause and journal how Jesus' words had an impact on
you today.

Reaching Forward with a Whole Heart

At times, we can be our own worst enemy. We may block forward
momentum by subjecting ourselves to personal condemnation. We're
not quite ready to let ourselves off the hook or let loose of our self-
disgust. We erect barricades that block us from receiving grace.
On some level, we believe that Jesus welcomes others but that we're
untouchable. We might keep trying or give up and camouflage our
pain. We might engage in destructive behavior or inflict cruel punish-
ment on ourselves.

Henri Nouwen wrote,

One of the greatest challenges of the spiritual life is to
receive forgiveness. There is something in us humans that
keeps us clinging to our sins and prevents us from letting God erase our past and offer us a completely new

beginning. . . . Receiving forgiveness requires a total will-ingness to let God be God and do all the healing, restoring, and renewing.[7]

What thoughts or feelings do Nouwen's words provoke?

Is there any unforgiveness of self that stands in your way or keeps you from moving forward in freedom?

Look up the following verses and read them aloud:

- Romans 8:1
- Romans 8:31-39
- Romans 10:3-4
- Ephesians 2:8
- Hebrews 10:17-18
- Hebrews 10:22-23

If one particular verse seems to command your attention or shout freedom to your heart, write it out here and dwell on it. Ask Jesus to cause the truth of the verse to make a home in your heart.

If you sense any condemnation or self-recrimination, appeal to Jesus, asking Him to lift it from your spirit. Choose a note card and write something like this on it:

> Because of Jesus, I am free. He does not condemn me, and because I am in Christ Jesus, all voices of condemnation, including my own, are no longer valid. I forgive myself for _____. I'm covered completely and eternally by the precious blood of Jesus. He has saved me completely. Nothing can ever separate me from the love of God in Christ Jesus. I choose to embrace the truth in God's Word and walk in freedom.

Place this card in your Bible, and as you read it throughout the week, imagine yourself reaching out to touch the cloak of Jesus. Release your battle to Him. Ask Jesus to sink each word into your mind, heart, and body.

Legacy of Redemption

As we live each day with a posture of reaching toward Jesus, He weaves all the messy threads into a beautiful tapestry of redemption and grace. Though He doesn't necessarily remove the consequences of our past actions or of others who have touched us, He does graciously restore the years the locusts have eaten (see Joel 2:25). For example, reality for me involves interacting with an ex-husband, raising three sons in a blended family, and the knowledge that there's a daughter out there I do not yet know. Still, I see my merciful Master leading me forward and shining the light on a redemptive pathway. Through it all, He provides a legacy of grace, healing, and a love that covers a multitude of sins (see 1 Peter 4:8).

The apostle Paul also knew the wonder of living in God's restorative grace. He accepted the fullness of forgiveness without minimizing the depths of sin from which he was rescued. Read over these portions of Paul's words, taken from *The Message*:

> Here's a word you can take to heart and depend on: Jesus Christ came into the world to save sinners. I'm proof—Public Sinner Number One—of someone who could never have made it apart from sheer mercy. And now he shows me off—evidence of his endless patience—to those who are right on the edge of trusting him forever. (1 Timothy 1:15-16)

> I'm not saying that I have this all together, that I have it made. But I am well on my way, reaching out for Christ, who has so wondrously reached out for me. Friends don't get me wrong: By no means do I count myself an expert in all of this, but I've got my eye on the goal, where God is beckoning us onward—to Jesus. I'm off and running, and I'm not turning back. (Philippians 3:12-14)

What invitation might Jesus be extending to you through these verses?

What legacy are you living and leaving as you embrace undivided freedom in Jesus?

Reflect

None of us is required to live chained down and walled in by past pain or present struggle. Because of Jesus, our hearts don't need to stay fragmented; we're released to embrace life. In the movie *Shawshank Redemption*, Tim Robbins plays a character wrongly imprisoned for years who finally escapes. He emerges from a sewage pipe shedding his polluted prison uniform, washes himself in the river, and steps into new clothes and a new life. Realization of his freedom dances across his face as he gazes at the expanse of sky above him.

What would your personal freedom scene include?

- Wiggling your toes in the sand
- Drawing deep breaths of fresh air
- Plunging into the water
- Singing at the top of your lungs
- Shouting for joy
- Trying to embrace the sky
- Twirling
- Resting quietly
- Other _____

What would you shed? What would you plunge into? What might you taste or feel?

What impact will freedom have on your relationship with Jesus? What impact will it have on your relationship with others?

Respond

As the focus of this week comes to a close, I pray an opening to freedom has been exposed. Try purposefully greeting each new morning exalting the Lord Jesus. Revel in His grace. Let joy explode and enfold you as you seek the face of and worship the only true Deliverer. Please join me in responding to the amazing love of Jesus by praying the following prayer based on Psalm 34:1-8:

> *I will extol You, Lord, at all times; Your praise*
> *will always be on my lips. My soul will boast in*
> *You, Lord; let the afflicted hear and rejoice. May*
> *they glorify You, Lord, with me; may we all exalt*
> *Your name together. I sought You, Lord, and You*
> *answered me; You delivered me from all my fears.*

As I look to You, I am radiant and my face is never covered with shame. Though I'm a poor woman, I called on You, Lord, and You heard me; You saved me out of all my troubles. May You encamp around me and deliver me. I've tasted and seen that You, Lord, are good; I'm blessed as I take refuge in You. Amen.

Shaped by Perfect Love

Settle into a comfortable position and quiet your heart for a few minutes, taking time to notice your breathing. Slowly inhale and release the air, asking the Lord to take you by the hand and draw you close. As you savor the nearness of Jesus, read this excerpt from *The Velveteen Rabbit* with the vulnerability of a child:

"What is real?" asked the toy Rabbit one day, when they were lying side by side near the nursery fender before Nana came to tidy the room. "Does it mean having things that buzz inside you and a stick-out handle?" "Real isn't how you are made," said the Skin Horse. "It's a thing that happens to you. When a child loves you for a long, long time, not just to play with, but REALLY loves you, then you become Real."[1]

How would you have answered the toy rabbit's question?

Try to describe a time when you noticed love unveiling authenticity in your own or another's life.

Ponder Scripture

The fear of human opinion disables;
trusting in GOD protects you from that.
— PROVERBS 29:25, MSG

For years I lived with unnecessary disability, living for the approval of others. The image I created of myself took on a life of its own, and I trembled at what might happen if I permitted myself to let it go. At times, I performed in order to impress, yet when it seemed I'd succeeded, I came away ashamed and empty. Sometimes I even refused to serve or use my abilities for fear of acting with wrong motivation. I spent a lot of time and effort trying to keep everyone around me happy. But when I contemplated the possibility of a different way of life, I'd ask myself, *What if I'm real and no one likes me?*

How have you also experienced fear of displeasing others? Which of these do you fear?

- Exposure
- Rejection
- Insignificance
- Loss of connection
- Loss of status
- Other _____

In the midst of my tangling daily with the tendency to please everyone, the Lord stepped into the fray and surprised me. I was reading through the book of Acts when I encountered Jesus in a new way.

Please read Acts 3:1-10. You may be wondering what this has to do with people pleasing, but it was in this passage that the Lord uncovered my heart and then covered my pain with His healing love. Based on that experience, I created an imaginary conversation with a good friend that I'd like to share with you.

Rita: "I've been reading in Acts, so I read Acts 3:1-10 and became a part of the story."

Friend: "Which part did you take?"

Rita: "I became the crippled beggar who got placed outside the temple courts at the gate called Beautiful. The beggar asked Peter and John for money, and they gave him healing instead. Then the beggar jumped for joy and everyone praised God."

Friend: "How did it feel to become the beggar?"

Rita: "I really identified with the beggar. I realized that I've been crippled by fear and want to enter into a gate called Beautiful; I long to be someone of worth. I try so hard to get there, but I've been asking for what I thought I needed, just like the beggar. He asked for money and I've been asking for approval. What is better is what was given: healing from a crippling disability and the ability to walk and leap for joy in this new life God has given me. I have worth in Him and want to walk in it. I want to be someone who inspires wonder and amazement, like the cripple, but not in terms of being amazed by me. I want to be someone who shows the wonder of what God can do. I want to be a living invitation to relationship with the Source of life and worth."

Friend: "How did the beggar become an invitation to wonder and amazement?"

Rita: (*thinking quietly for a few moments*) "By receiving. I desperately want to receive my identity and live in it. I'm praying about how to do that."

Friend: "And what have you heard to this point?"

Rita: "There's a verse the Lord's been calling me to really believe and live in. 'As the Father has loved me, so have I loved you. Now remain in my love' (John 15:9). I think I need to stay near Jesus and ask for grace to receive safety, love, identity, and authenticity."

When you look at your relationship with Jesus and others, what have you seen as your most pressing need?

Is there a possibility that Jesus has a greater treasure to lavish on you? What might that be?

Consider reading through Acts 3:1-10 and becoming part of the story. Which part will you take? What about that role lures you?

In your journal experiment with writing your own imaginary dialogue. Pour out your heart and imagine the response of a dear friend.

A Safe Unveiling

Like the Velveteen Rabbit, we learn to be real in an atmosphere of relentless love.

Close your eyes and place yourself in an atmosphere you've always associated with warmth and welcome. Breathe the air and rest for a few moments. Linger there as you meditate on the following passages:

> This is what the high and lofty One says—
>> he who lives forever, whose name is holy:
> "I live in a high and holy place,
>> but also with him who is contrite and lowly in spirit,
> to revive the spirit of the lowly
>> and to revive the heart of the contrite." (Isaiah 57:15)

> A bruised reed he will not break,
>> and a smoldering wick he will not snuff out. (Matthew 12:20)

> I'm absolutely convinced that nothing—nothing living or dead, angelic or demonic, today or tomorrow, high or low, thinkable or unthinkable—absolutely *nothing* can get

between us and God's love because of the way that Jesus our Master has embraced us. (Romans 8:38-39, MSG)

God is love. When we take up permanent residence in a life of love, we live in God and God lives in us. This way, love has the run of the house, becomes at home and mature in us, so that we're free of worry on Judgment Day—our standing in the world is identical with Christ's. There is no room in love for fear. Well-formed love banishes fear. Since fear is crippling, a fearful life—fear of death, fear of judgment—is one not yet fully formed in love.

We, though, are going to love—love and be loved. Fist we were loved, now we love. He loved us first. (1 John 4:17-19, MSG)

What common threads run through these passages?

What phrase or theme is soothing to your spirit?

We're invited to make our home in love. What characterizes that love?

List any ways that dwelling in Jesus' love frees you to become real.

Brainstorm how you can learn to linger more at home in love throughout each day.

A True Identity

In the film *Runaway Bride*, Julia Roberts plays a character named Maggie who melds her personality and preferences to that of her current fiancé and then, as if some survival instinct kicks in, leaves each of her prospective grooms at the altar. Her loss of self and personal preferences becomes evident even in the way her eggs are prepared. With the health-conscious guy, it's egg whites only; with another, it's eggs Benedict, and so on. She's confronted with her behavior and, in a scene near the end, has her own private egg tasting to determine what she does and does not like.

Is there any way that you tend to melt into others and lose who you are?

Like Maggie, we may walk through days so focused on finding approval, gaining acceptance, or working hard to impress others that we never really figure out our true identity. We create an image we hope will make us more palatable to others, only to realize we've forgotten who we really are. It's as if pieces of our hearts are gouged out, and empty spaces are filled with foreign particles that seep deeper and deeper until we can't even tell where the holes are.

Read over the following excerpt from Simon Tugwell, noting any thoughts, ideas, and feelings it provokes:

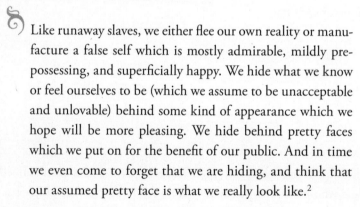

Like runaway slaves, we either flee our own reality or manufacture a false self which is mostly admirable, mildly prepossessing, and superficially happy. We hide what we know or feel ourselves to be (which we assume to be unacceptable and unlovable) behind some kind of appearance which we hope will be more pleasing. We hide behind pretty faces which we put on for the benefit of our public. And in time we even come to forget that we are hiding, and think that our assumed pretty face is what we really look like.[2]

Becoming real can be a scary prospect. Draw near to Jesus. Ask Him to cradle your heart as He shows you blind spots or ways you may be hiding. Be gentle with yourself, remembering "that he who began a good work in you will carry it on to completion until the day of Christ Jesus" (Philippians 1:6). Be still and listen. If something comes to mind, write it down here or in your journal and let it prompt prayer.

Ask Jesus for courage to continue becoming all He has for you to be.

David Benner wrote,

 There is no true life apart from relationship to God. Therefore there can be no true self apart from this relationship. The foundation of our identity resides in our life-giving relationship with the Source of life. Any identity that exists apart from this relationship is an illusion."[3]

Even in times when we've lost sight of our true self, the Lord sees us and can help us see who we are in Him.

Go to the mirror of God's Word and fill in some of your identifying characteristics in Christ.

Scripture Reference	Identifying Characteristics
Romans 8:1-2	
2 Corinthians 5:17-21	
Ephesians 1:3	
Ephesians 1:4	

Ephesians 1:5-6	
Ephesians 1:7	
Ephesians 1:11	
Ephesians 1:13	
Ephesians 2:6	
Ephesians 2:10	
Ephesians 3:12	

Which, if any, passage leaped off the page when you read it?

What is it about that passage that grabbed your attention?

Choose one or two of the listed scriptures to focus on, keeping them near your mirror to remind you each day of who you are. Begin and end your day proclaiming your true identity. Once your initial selections settle in your heart, prayerfully add more, repeating the process. Margaret Becker sings, "Slowly I'm becoming who I am."[4] Jesus is present in the process. Welcome the becoming. Celebrate when you're reminded of who you truly are.

Real Connection

One point of clarification is important before we continue. In referring to people pleasing, I'm not suggesting it's wrong to receive affirmation from another. C. S. Lewis said,

> The child who is patted on the back for doing a lesson well, the woman whose beauty is praised by her lover, the saved soul to whom Christ says, 'Well done,' are pleased and ought to be. For here the pleasure lies . . . in the fact that you have pleased someone you wanted (and rightly wanted) to please.[5]

Growth in our capacity to give and receive love includes affirmation and enhances connection. It is when our desire for approval rules us, our pride erects an image or demands recognition, or we make approval an empty cistern from which no water is available (see Jeremiah 2:13) that it becomes a barrier to oneness. When we are preoccupied with what others think of us and try to manage interactions in a desperate effort to assuage the loneliness underneath, our hearts splinter.

Henri Nouwen said it like this:

> Why is it that many parties and friendly get-togethers leave us so empty and sad? Maybe even there the deep-seated and often unconscious competition between people prevents them from revealing themselves to each other and from

establishing relationships that last longer than the party itself.[6]

When was the last time you felt alone in a crowd?

If you get caught in the battle between authentic living and people pleasing, which of the following are you most likely to do?

- ✦ Feel you must always please others first
- ✦ Feel fake
- ✦ Say yes even when your heart says no
- ✦ Feel resentful
- ✦ Fear becoming selfish
- ✦ Sense you're settling for only caricatures of relationships
- ✦ Other _____

Living a life of love from the heart is risky but, in the end, a risk worth taking. Sometimes when others are pleased, there's a temporary sense that we're accepted, but it never seems to be quite enough. Fears aren't magically alleviated. Even when approval seems within our grasp, it's lonely for the real person inside. We want to feel known and not settle for something less than genuine love.

Please read Romans 15:7, 1 Corinthians 13, and James 5:16. How would you apply the kind of authentic love detailed in these passages to the development of relationships?

Optional Exercise

Pretend Jesus is the friend sitting across from you. Tell Him the details of what happens in your heart when you try to connect with others. Tell Him about your loneliness. Try recording your conversation with Him as dialogue; then share that dialogue with a trusted friend and pray together about any issues raised.

There is a place where becoming real and seeking to please can safely coincide. In Jesus' presence, we are completely known, yet He bathes us in unconditional love. When we come naked before the Lord Jesus, He clothes us. When we seek to live for His pleasure, we become a little more of who we were made to be each day. Come to Him and ask Him to replace any dividing desire for others' approval in your heart with the desire to be 100 percent His. Pray along with these verses from Psalms:

> Show me your ways, O Lord,
>   teach me your paths;
> guide me in your truth and teach me,
>   for you are God my Savior,
>   and my hope is in you all day long. (25:4-5)

> Teach me your way, O Lord,
>   and I will walk in your truth;
> give me an undivided heart,
>   that I may fear your name.
> I will praise you, O Lord my God, with all my heart;
>   I will glorify your name forever.
> For great is your love toward me;
>   you have delivered me from the depths of the grave.
>   (86:11-13)

Reflect

Masquerade! Paper faces on parade . . .
Masquerade! Hide your face, so the world will never find you.
— "Masquerade," *Phantom of the Opera*

These lyrics tease me with an illusion of a safe existence. I'm tempted to hide my heart away so that it cannot be broken. Instead, in the arms of Jesus, I'm learning to identify my masks as the thin paper shields they really are and venture out more to honestly extend myself to others.

Draw a few masks and name the ones you are most comfortable wearing. Some possibilities may be:

- Clown
- Pain free
- Superwoman
- Thick-skinned
- No needs
- Doormat
- Perfect
- Ultraspiritual
- Other _____

As you consider the masks, try to identify what is hiding beneath. Take that vulnerability to Jesus and bask in His amazing love. Reflect on what Jesus might be inviting you to in that moment. Then ask Him to keep a tight hold on your heart as He reveals opportunities in the coming week for you to become real. In the safety of His arms, hear Him beckon you to live authentically and restfully through Sandra Wilson's reflection on Scripture:

Grace to you and peace are my gifts to you and all my children. You have been seeking grace (a favored status) from people, believing it will bring peace. It never does. Only entering more and more deeply into the reality of my grace will bring the genuine peace of heart you are dying for.
I already died for it.
And I rose so you would know it's true.
And I have the power to make it true for you.
Hear me.
Believe me.
Learn to rest in the peace of my grace.[7]

Respond

During the bombing raids of World War II, thousands of children were orphaned and left to starve. The fortunate ones were rescued and placed in refugee camps where they received food and good care, but many of these children who had lost so much could not sleep at night. They feared waking up to find themselves once again homeless and without food. Nothing seemed to reassure them. Finally someone hit upon the idea of giving each child a piece of bread to hold at bedtime. Holding their bread, these children could finally sleep in peace. All through the night, the bread reminded them, "Today I ate and I will eat again tomorrow."[8]

There is an ancient spiritual practice called the examen that invites us to reflect on the ways God is at work in our daily lives and relationships. Often this is done by noting highs and lows of the day or by asking ourselves one or two simple questions that help us review our day. In a way similar to that of the children orphaned during World War II, we end our day with the reassurance that just as the Lord was present in our lives today, He will be there tomorrow. We are encouraged to embrace and gain awareness of the Lord's nourishing activity in our lives. In addition, there's opportunity to release difficult moments and receive grace.

This week, consider experimenting with this practice. At the end of the day, quietly invite the Lord to guide your thinking as you engage in the discipline of examen through these questions: *When did I feel most masked with God or others today? When did I feel most real with God or others?*

Hold each moment before Jesus and ask Him to help you glean insight and nourishment for your continuing journey to authenticity. Celebrate each moment of authenticity as you reflect on your day.

Awake to His Voice

A few years ago, I participated in a training exercise designed to offer a glimpse into the thinking of a young woman wrestling with an unplanned pregnancy. The focus of the training highlighted the struggle involved in sifting through competing voices in the midst of a crisis. One participant played the part of the young woman and was seated in the middle of the group. Others surrounded her, taking on a variety of roles, such as her mom, her dad, the father of her unborn baby, a friend, a teacher, her boss, societal opinion, and so on. On the count of three, all the voices began shouting opinions, giving advice, and expressing thoughts. When the room became silent again, the woman in the middle shared that even though she was role-playing, she experienced a sense of gut-wrenching vulnerability and confusion. She made such comments as "I couldn't hear my own voice," "I couldn't think or reason," "I felt attacked," and "I felt split in a thousand directions."

Pivotal times of decision making might not characterize our typical day. Still, there's constant competition for our attention. It's challenging to wake up to a silent place where we hear our Beloved speak. It's as if we must continually fend off a multitude of voices trying to embed themselves in our hearts like secret agents of distortion. We fight the noise that threatens to lure us away or to block out the voice of Jesus.

Describe your personal fight to hear the Lord in the mundane or the momentous. What voices crowd your heart?

Isaiah 50:4 says, "He wakens me morning by morning, wakens my ear to listen like one being taught." Ask the Lord to awaken your heart fully to His voice. Pray for ears to hear and for a shelter of quiet. Embrace a time of stillness as you enter into this week's study. Sit comfortably for a minute or two. Take all the time you need to become quiet. Play a favorite worship song or instrumental music, listen to birds, or simply be silent. Set aside each thought that intrudes and say, "I'm listening, Lord."

Wait until you are ready, and then move on the next section.

Ponder Scripture

Why is it that when we speak to God we are said to be praying,
but when God speaks to us we are said to be schizophrenic?
— LILY TOMLIN IN *THE SEARCH FOR SIGNS OF*
INTELLIGENT LIFE IN THE UNIVERSE

If the Lord miraculously spoke to me in an audible voice, I think I would fall to my face trembling. I don't hear Him speak with my physical ears, but He does speak. His voice is real. Read the following passages aloud as if you were auditioning for a play based on Scripture. Roll the words around, finding different ways of phrasing each thought. Explore the tone of God's voice. For example, do you hear power, tenderness, calm, authority, soothing, or energy? Briefly jot down any thoughts after each reading.

> God said, "Let there be light," and there was light.
> (Genesis 1:3)

> When the LORD saw that he had gone over to look, God called to him from within the bush, "Moses, Moses!"
> And Moses said, "Here I am."
> "Do not come any closer," God said. "Take off your sandals, for the place where you are standing is holy ground." (Exodus 3:4-5)

> Fear not, for I have redeemed you;
>   I have summoned you by name; you are mine.
> When you pass through the waters,
>   I will be with you;
> and when you pass through the rivers,
>   they will not sweep over you.
> When you walk through the fire,
>   you will not be burned;

the flames will not set you ablaze. (Isaiah 43:1-2)

Immediately Jesus reached out his hand and caught him. "You of little faith," he said, "why did you doubt?" (Matthew 14:31)

O Jerusalem, Jerusalem, you who kill the prophets and stone those sent to you, how often I have longed to gather your children together, as a hen gathers her chicks under her wings, but you were not willing. (Matthew 23:37)

"Martha, Martha," the Lord answered, "you are worried and upset about many things, but only one thing is needed. Mary has chosen what is better, and it will not be taken away from her." (Luke 10:41-42)

As the Father has loved me, so have I loved you. Now remain in my love. (John 15:9)

As he neared Damascus on his journey, suddenly a light from heaven flashed around him. He fell to the ground and heard a voice say to him, "Saul, Saul, why do you persecute me?" (Acts 9:3-4)

Here I am! I stand at the door and knock. If anyone hears my voice and opens the door, I will come in and eat with him, and he with me. (Revelation 3:20)

Which tone of voice do you tend to assume the Lord uses when addressing your heart? Which tones do you feel most in need of today?

An Intimate Call

Whose phone call can bring tears to your eyes or a smile to your face the moment you recognize the voice on the other end of the line? What makes the voice familiar?

Please read John 10:3-5. Some time ago, I read a story about two shepherds who decided to shelter their sheep in the same cave for the night, yet there was no confusion in the morning sorting out all the sheep. All it took was for the shepherds to give their unique call and their sheep came running to them. The call of Jesus is unique too. I'm still dazzled by the thought of Jesus being interested enough in each of us to know and call us by name. We're not a generic group of sheep, known as sheep number 3,126,467. There's nothing impersonal about how Jesus chooses to speak.

How have you spent time recently listening for Jesus to call you by name?

Often when I hear my name spoken, I hear so much more than a word. As a child, when my mom used my first and middle name—Rita June—especially with the volume turned up a little, I knew I was in some kind of trouble. Other times, I've heard my name called with excitement, exasperation, tenderness, and love. What do you hear in the call of Jesus?

Author Jan Harris suggested that the call of Jesus is full of purposeful passion.

The author of The Cloud says, "The eternal love of God . . . could not bear to let you go on living so . . . far from him." Imagine—the Lord could not bear it! So, "he awakened desire within you, and . . . drew you close to himself." Has God awakened desire in you?[1]

How would you respond to her question?

At times, exploring places of unspeakable natural beauty has awakened my ears to the voice of the Lord. I listen to His handiwork, and His creativity draws me near.

Psalm 19:1-4 proclaims:

God's glory is on tour in the skies,
     God-craft on exhibit across the horizon.
Madame Day holds classes every morning,
     Professor Night lectures each evening.

Their words aren't heard,
     their voices aren't recorded,
But their silence fills the earth:
     unspoken truth is spoken everywhere. (MSG)

When you linger over the voice of the Lord in nature, what message do you hear?

What is most likely to drift into the ears of your spirit or cause you to sit up and listen to Jesus' voice?

- A baby cooing
- A sunset
- Laughter
- A couple in love
- Snow falling
- A magnificent painting
- A garden
- Blazing colors in the fall
- The sound of a harp
- A beautiful operatic voice
- Other _____

How would it shape your day to be aware of and attuned to Jesus' voice?

Creating Space to Hear

> *And while in this silence, God pours into you a deep, inward love. This experience of love is one that will fill and permeate your whole being. . . . This love which the Lord pours into your depths is the beginning of an indescribable blessedness.*
> — JEANNE GUYON, *EXPERIENCING THE DEPTHS OF JESUS CHRIST*

Life seems to rush past and swirl around me. I need to rescue some time to linger. One silent interlude drew me to the Lover of my soul in a new way. At that time, I held an emotionally demanding job but thought I could also handle hosting my family for Christmas. I got caught up in my attempt to make each detail special. Everyone had a good time, but at the end of the holiday, I realized I hadn't entered into the wonder and rest of Christmas. I had nothing left. I was exhausted—depleted mentally, emotionally, physically, and spiritually.

My weariness prompted me to literally head for the hills. I drove into the mountains west of Denver to a silent prayer and retreat house, hoping to regain some energy. The discipline of silence was honored even in the dining room of this facility. Wonderful smells invited me to come and receive my dinner. At first I felt silly and a little lonely sitting by myself at a table for four eating in complete silence. At almost the same moment, Jesus called to my heart, embracing me with a tender and solicitous voice: "Rita, you are not alone. I'm here with you at the table. This is time for you to be cared for and fed. Are you getting enough to eat?" The tears mingled with my dinner, and throughout the remainder of my retreat, I communed with my Lord, knowing restoration in His presence. Refreshment became indelibly imprinted on my spirit.

Periodically, Jesus interrupts my often self-made chaos through Scripture, saying, "Rita, be still." Please read Psalm 46:10, Psalm

131:2, and Habakkuk 2:20. Why do you think God wants us to embrace silence?

Dallas Willard commented, "Silence is frightening because it strips us as nothing else does, throwing us upon the stark realities of our life."[2] What do you see as the risk of silence for you?

Will you take one step past your fear and experiment with creating space for silence? When driving, keep the radio or music turned off and remain quiet. Then process in your journal how it felt to leave that space of time uncluttered with noise.

Another Kind of Silence

A few years ago, a friend I greatly respect as a woman of character and a seeker of the Lord shared her struggle with the silence of God. She was spending regular time in silence and hearing nothing. Exhausting all the reasons for God's silence she could come up with, she came to a place of rest in the middle of what she called "a dark night of the soul." Even though she wasn't hearing from the Lord, she sensed a strange holding still inside, a sense that this interval was somehow okay. During this season and as the sound of His care began to filter into her spirit, she wrote some beautiful music that carried the Lord's voice to others.

I cannot presume to know what the Lord is up to when He is silent, but I know He is still there. If, like my friend, you feel as though someone has turned the volume down or even off on God's voice, I hope you will find some encouragement from her story. Consider pausing and journaling some of your hopes, dreams, and prayers for your future with the Lord.

Let these words of Psalm 27:14 penetrate your spirit:

> Wait for the LORD,
>   be strong and take heart
>   and wait for the LORD.

Awakening to Scripture

At a conference a friend and I were attending together, we were instructed to find a quiet spot and interact with Psalm 63. We were told to leave behind our tendency to skim for information, read on automatic, and recite words to finish a task. Some contemplative exercises were suggested, and off we went to our own corners. My friend emerged from her first experience of reading Scripture in this new way with her face glowing, her voice colored by awe, saying, "That was amazing."

In a similar way, let's relish the presence of the Lord as we interact with and enter into Scripture. Let's try to leave behind preconceived notions of the passage. Approach John 20:1-2,10-18 expectantly. Read aloud slowly and deliberately. Resist the urge to go quickly over any sections because they are familiar. Try to read the passage as if it were new to you. What words or phrases stand out to you?

Keeping in mind that Jesus delivered Mary Magdalene from seven demons (see Mark 16:9), imagine her devotion to Jesus. Read the passage again and sit quietly, letting the scene play out in your mind. Place yourself in the midst of the sights, sounds, and smells. Allow yourself a few minutes of silence and record any impressions, thoughts, and feelings here or in your journal.

Now choose one or more of the following exercises:

- Pretend you are Mary rising before dark and on your way to the tomb. In what mood did you awaken? What is going through your mind?
- Pretend you are one of the two angels in white watching this whole scene. What impresses you?
- Mary was distraught. How would it feel to believe that the Lord who delivered you was gone forever? Is it possible she believed she would never again hear Jesus speak her name? Now with those emotions in mind, reread verses 15-18. What is your reaction?
- Mull over reasons for Jesus to choose the questions He asked in verse 15?
- Mary heard her name and clung to Jesus. She must have wanted to stay right there forever, but Jesus had something better in mind. Is there any way in which you are hanging on that expresses your expectation but Jesus wants you to let go so you can receive His best?
- Think through any invitation that Jesus extends to you through this passage. How do you intend to respond?

- As a woman, how would you feel going to the disciples with Jesus' message? Mark 16:11 says, "When they heard that Jesus was alive and that she had seen him, they did not believe it." How, if at all, would it affect you if your words were met with disbelief?

Reread John 20:10-18. Draw a symbol or illustration that represents how God is speaking to you, making it as simple or elaborate as you wish. Write a prayer based on your interaction with this passage.

Reflect

During the breaks at a women's conference I attended, the concourses were congested with hundreds of women trying to make their way to the restrooms, the concession stands, or book tables. Voices intermingled as they laughed, cried, and discussed anything and everything. If you stood still and listened, you heard what sounded like a huge group of chattering geese on a lakeshore. I stepped into an elevator, and as the doors closed, one woman drew a deep breath and said, "Listen, silence." It was as if someone turned the volume off. For that short elevator ride, we honored the quiet.

Like those concourses, our lives are often inundated with noise. It could be wildly fun noise, necessary noise, or overwhelming noise. In any case, we all need space to breathe, be still before the Lord, and honor the quiet. An intriguing practice that can be helpful in observing silence is the night watch. As Dallas Willard mentioned, "Many have learned to rise for a time in the middle of the night—to break the night's sleep in half in order to experience such silence."[3] Others have combined rising during the night with a prayerful watching for morning to begin. One possible way to engage in a night watch is to rise before the dawn, nurse a cup of coffee (or your beverage of choice), sit facing a window or outside if possible, and watch for the night to end.

Experiment with your own version of a night watch. Plan a day that will work for you and rise to share the quiet with the Lord. One way to begin and focus your time is to read from Psalms. Here are a couple of verses you could get started with:

> You have made known to me the path of life;
>> you will fill me with joy in your presence,
>> with eternal pleasures at your right hand. (16:11)

> I pray to GOD—my life a prayer—
>> and wait for what he'll say and do.
> My life's on the line before God, my Lord,
>> waiting and watching till morning,
>> waiting and watching till morning. (130:5-6, MSG)

Sit back, open your ears, and enjoy watching for the coming day in the presence of the Lord. Take some time, if you wish, to record any insights or impressions here or in your journal.

Respond

God is a person, and in the deep of His mighty nature He thinks, wills, enjoys, feels, loves, desires and suffers as any other person may. In making Himself known to us He stays by the familiar pattern of personality. He communicates with us through the avenues of our minds, our wills and our emotions. The continuous and unembarrassed interchange of love and thought between God and the soul of the redeemed man is the throbbing heart of New Testament religion.

— A. W. TOZER

Please begin praying with me and continue on as you are led. Culminate your prayer with a time of listening attentively for the voice of your Beloved.

> *Lord, the gift of knowing You, of hearing You, is amazing. Coach us as we learn to recognize Your voice. Empower us to still competing voices and offer You our undivided attention. How we long to know You more, to love You more, and to stay nestled in this "interchange of love and thought."*

Adoring Gaze

Open the eyes of my heart, Lord. I want to see you.
— Paul Baloche

Sometimes life grows blurry and it's easy to slip into a pattern of sleepwalking through the day. I find myself crying out to God, "I need You to open my eyes, to focus them and bring true color and shape to my vision. I'm stunned that You seek to establish eye contact with me. Don't let me miss Your brilliance today."

Please join me in cherishing the gift of knowing Jesus by proclaiming the words of the following psalm:

I bless God every chance I get;
my lungs expand with his praise.

I live and breathe God;
if things aren't going well, hear this and be happy:

Join me in spreading the news;
together let's get the word out.

God met me more than halfway,
he freed me from my anxious fears.

Look at him; give him your warmest smile.
Never hide your feelings from him.

When I was desperate, I called out,
and God got me out of a tight spot.

God's angel sets up a circle
of protection around us while we pray.

Open your mouth and taste, open your eyes and see — how good
    God is.
Blessed are you who run to him.

Worship God if you want the best;
worship opens doors to all his goodness. (34:1-9, MSG)

What would it look like for you to begin the day looking at Jesus and giving Him your warmest smile?

Ponder Scripture

The next day John saw Jesus coming toward him, and said, "Behold the Lamb of God who takes away the sin of the world!"

— JOHN 1:29, NKJV

Behold is not a word we use much. We're more likely to say, "Wow, check out that sunset" or "Look at that face," but somehow those phrases don't fit in John 1:29. *Behold* sounds majestic, important, full of wonder. The Greek word *emblepo*, translated "behold," implies more than a casual glance or quick notice; it "expresses earnest looking"[1] and means "to look in the face, fix the eyes upon, stare at."[2]

What would it be like for you to earnestly look into the face of the Lamb of God?

What happens to the scattered places in your heart when you gaze at Jesus, who voluntarily took your sin on Himself?

As a worship leader, I don't always recognize when someone is looking into the face of their Savior, but sometimes a countenance is transformed by a glimpse of the Lord. When I'm privileged to see adoration take shape, I feel as though I've been let into a private holy place. Tears might roll down a radiant face or features might reflect utter serenity, and suddenly I no longer see that person: I see the wonder of a beautiful Savior, and I, too, am led in worship.

Scripture is filled with picture-perfect moments that invite us in and call us to stop to worship. C. S. Lewis said, "We do not merely want to *see* beauty. We want something else which can hardly be put in words—to be united with the beauty we see, to pass into it, to receive it into ourselves, to bathe in it, to become part of it."[3] As you look upon the following verses, I pray you'll be led into a deeper stare, one that plunges you into consuming love for the Lord.

Please read Isaiah 6:1-4. Which details of the Lord's awesome majesty capture your imagination first?

- The high throne
- The train of His robe filling the temple
- The winged seraphs
- The seraphs' call
- The shaking doorposts and thresholds
- The smoke filling the temple

Continue on in Isaiah 6, reading through verse 8. The *New Bible Dictionary* describes *seraphim* as divine worship leaders extolling the character of God.[4] Imagine the power and intensity of the cry "holy, holy, holy" shaking the temple and filling it with smoke. How might you react to seeing a seraph?

When Isaiah saw the Lord, he also saw himself clearly. He knew he couldn't stand in the presence of God, but the Lord graciously provided a way of atonement. Visualize the burning coal coming toward him. Notice as it touches his lips, preparing him for service. Scripture doesn't tell us if it left a physical scar, but Isaiah's life was marked permanently. His life was transformed.

Jesus bore the scars that transform our lives. We gain the honor of entering into the Holy of Holies because of Him. We come directly to the throne room of the Almighty God.

We can now—without hesitation—walk right up to God, into "the Holy Place." Jesus has cleared the way by the blood of his sacrifice, acting as our priest before God. The "curtain" into God's presence is his body.

So let's *do* it—full of belief, confident that we're presentable inside and out. (Hebrews 10:19-22, MSG)

Go behind the curtain today. Let the nail-scarred hand of Jesus cup your face and tilt it to gaze upon His beauty. Behold Him. Linger in the throne room.

How are you changed after spending time in the inner sanctuary with Jesus?

Love Poured Out

Turn to Luke 7:36-50 and visualize the scene as you read. When the woman learned that Jesus was there, she knew or fully recognized who was having dinner at Simon's house.[5] She saw Him as one worthy of passionate, costly worship. Before she could pour out the perfume, her heart became liquid, falling at the feet of Jesus. She wiped His feet with her hair and kissed them repeatedly. This was no proper or stilted action. This wasn't a demonstration in groveling but in seeing the Lord and herself more clearly. She poured out her heart completely and went away changed. She looked at Jesus, "the Lamb of God who takes away the sin of the world" (John 1:26, NKJV), and He saw her too.

Reflect on this woman's deep love for Jesus, a love expressed even in the face of scorn. She saw Him as worthy of worship, and He saw her need. Can you imagine the pounding in her heart when she saw the love of a Savior in His eyes?

Try to illustrate this scene (stick figures are okay).

Imagine you are arriving at a dinner and Jesus is there. What do you see when you look at Him? How are you affected when He sees you?

What is your posture as you behold Jesus?

- Standing in awe
- Kneeling at His feet
- Sitting in silence
- Facedown before Him
- Hands lifted in praise
- Other _____

What brings your heart to this posture today?

A Visual Refuge

Where do you focus your eyes when life gets challenging? As I've been writing this study, my husband and I have been facing a disease that threatens to cripple him or take his life. He's making progress, but evidence of the disease is still a daily reminder of where we've been and tempers our tendency to say that all is well. Throughout this period of our lives, I've found that my eyes have a mind of their own. They sneak past my resolution not to borrow trouble for tomorrow and examine a whole lot of what-ifs. When I fail to stop them, my heart is twisted, pieced out, and full of anxiety. Jesus graciously draws my eye, saying, "Rita, over here, eyes on Me."

As an exercise to help you stay focused, mull over Hebrews 12:1-3. The *Amplified Bible* offers these phrases within this passage:

- "looking away [from all that will distract] to Jesus"
- "so that you may not grow weary or exhausted, losing heart and relaxing and fainting in your minds"

Is there any sense in which your eyes want to wander? What happens to your energy level, your heart, and your mind when your eyes drift? What helps you to fix your eyes on Jesus?

Kingdom Eyes

The more I gaze upon the beauty of Jesus and bask in the wonder that He sees me, the more He calls me to begin seeing the world with His eyes. I can gravitate automatically to a numbing self-focus, but Jesus has a way of readjusting my vision. At one point, He captured my attention when I least expected it through a scene in the movie *Titanic* that still haunts me. The ship has sunk and bodies fill the sea. Frozen faces like gray mannequins bob up and down in the water, some with grotesque smiles. Each man, woman, and child paralyzed and headed for certain death.

For me, those faces represent far more than computer-generated victims of a disaster at sea; they are the faces of people I pass by each day—people who need Jesus. They're people Jesus sees, people He wants me to see. Their faces scroll across my memory and the tears begin to flow. I weep at their pain. I weep at how easily I slip into a life of comfortable blindness, when all around me people are aching, some are dying. Driven to my knees, I pray, "Lord, forgive me. Transform my eyesight. Help me see." The answer to my prayer begins with this realization: I must look through the compassionate eyes of Jesus to see others with love and clarity. Apart from Him, my understanding is limited at best.

In Harper Lee's novel *To Kill a Mockingbird*, Atticus Finch says, "You'll never understand a man 'til you stand in his shoes and look at the world through his eyes."[6]

Take note of what Jesus sees. Try to look at the world through His eyes as you read the following verses:

When he saw the crowds, he had compassion on them, because they were harassed and helpless, like sheep without a shepherd. Then he said to his disciples, "The harvest is plentiful but the workers are few. Ask the Lord of the harvest, therefore, to send out workers into his harvest field." (Matthew 9:36-38)

As he approached the town gate, a dead person was being carried out—the only son of his mother, and she was a widow. And a large crowd from the town was with her. When the Lord saw her, his heart went out to her and he said, "Don't cry." (Luke 7:12-13)

People were also bringing babies to Jesus to have him touch them. When the disciples saw this, they rebuked them. But Jesus called the children to him and said, "Let the little children come to me, and do not hinder them, for the kingdom of God belongs to such as these." (Luke 18:15-16)

What do you see in the faces of those who surround you each day?

In what way might Jesus be adjusting your focus?

Respond in your journal to any change of focus or thoughts or feelings stirred up by the following quotes:

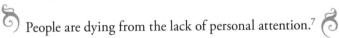 People are dying from the lack of personal attention.[7]

Giving needs not to be confined to money or material gifts, but I would like more people to give their hands to serve and their hearts to love—to recognize the poor in their own homes, towns and countries, and to reach out to them in love and compassion.[8]

I always explain to the sisters, "It is Christ you tend in the poor. It is his wounds you bathe, his sores you clean, his limbs you bandage. See beyond appearances, and hear the words Jesus pronounced long ago. They are still operative today: What you do to the least of mine you do it to me. When you serve the poor, you serve our Lord Jesus Christ."[9]

Please pray with me, opening your heart fully to see and act on what you see:

> *Lord, focus my eyes foremost on You. May every glance deepen my love for You. Let that love flow through me and overflow to all You put in my path. Let my life become an expression of the amazing love and grace You have lavished on my heart. Teach me to see others through Your eyes. Show me how You would have me act on what I see. Amen.*

Reflect

Deuteronomy 11:18 says, "Fix these words of mine in your hearts and minds; tie them as symbols on your hands and bind them on your foreheads." The Israelites were exhorted to sear into their memories God's interaction with them. We also benefit from reminders of the Lord's interaction with us, those holy encounters we can be so prone to forget.

Set aside some time to reflect on a moment when you beheld the Lord in a new way or when you were visually reminded of a truth. Choose one of the following exercises to help you reflect:

- Take your camera and spend some time capturing images that symbolize what you saw.
- Write a word picture or journal the details.
- Attempt to use color (crayons, paint, watercolors) to express your interaction with the Lord.
- Use clay or even Play-Doh to sculpt your moment and give it form.
- Immerse yourself in a piece of music (listening, playing an instrument, singing) that expresses how your heart was affected by seeing the Lord.
- Choose a different format of your own to capture your moment.

Respond

Even as astounded as we are when we catch a glimpse of Jesus, we know there's so much more in store. Those sightings of Jesus keep our eyes focused, waiting for the day when our vision will be complete. Let anticipation and longing wash over your spirit, uniting your heart in worship of Jesus.

> Now we see but a poor reflection as in a mirror; then we shall see face to face. Now I know in part; then I shall know fully, even as I am fully known. (1 Corinthians 13:12)

> No longer will there be any curse. The throne of God and of the Lamb will be in the city, and his servants will serve him. They will see his face, and his name will be on their foreheads. (Revelation 22:3-4)

These verses reveal our glorious future, but for now our hearts plead the lyrics of an old hymn:

> Jesus, the very thought of thee
> With sweetness fills my breast;
> But sweeter far thy face to see
> And in thy presence rest.[10]

Pour out your desire for the Lord. Hold your whole heart out to Him and ask Him to daily draw you close, clearing your vision so that you might know Him more.

Please pray with me and continue as you are led:

> *Lord Jesus, I'm in awe of You. I bow at Your feet in adoration. You are so beautiful, holy, and good. Please keep me seeking Your face. Capture and consume my whole heart with love for You. Touch my eyes. Help me see You more clearly each day. I long for that moment when I will see You face-to-face and know love as I've never known it before. Until then, Lord, let love for You pour through my life and spill out on others that they may see You too.*

Wholly Satisfied

Thou hast made us for Thyself, and our hearts are restless until they rest in Thee.

— AUGUSTINE OF HIPPO

Much of what I took in years ago during a sociology class on marriage and the family is a little vague now, but one particular day of class stands out. Most of my classmates were women in their early twenties. The class was asked to answer this question: "What do women deem most important or look for first when assessing a man as a potential husband?" Overwhelmingly, the answer was the guy's potential for plentiful financial resources. I sat surprised that the class would be so openly mercenary, but most of the women made no apology for their quest. They felt that a satisfying marriage required a man with an abundance of income. Their sentiments were echoed in a recent report I saw on a segment of the *Today* show. A number of women admitted they inspected a man's shoes for signs of expense or position before considering him worthy of dating.

What desires do you think are reflected in the class's answer?

Married or not, have you ever known someone who seems close to living a satisfied life? If so, describe that person.

If you were to give an estimate of your heart's satisfaction level in terms of percentages, what would it be?

Ponder Scripture

The American Heritage Dictionary defines *satisfaction* as "the fulfillment or gratification of a desire, need, or expectation."[1] What happens when we seek to fulfill competing or confusing desires or even shadows of our true desire? Our hearts churn, split, and settle for whatever we think may pacify or even silence our most demanding longings. David Benner referred to our desires being either "disordered" or "purified."

He suggested we sort them out by carefully noting their effects:

Ordered — or purified — desires expand me and connect me to others and the world in life-enhancing ways. Disordered desires suck me into myself and rather than adding vitality to life, leach it away. This is because ordered desires spring from willingness and surrender, while disordered ones are my willful attempt to arrange for my own happiness or fulfillment. When I desire nothing more than God alone, I experience a deep sense of well-being and connectedness. Paradoxically, this is a longing that leaves me feeling not empty but complete.[2]

What is your initial reaction to the idea of sorting out desires?

Please read John 4:7-29, keeping in mind that the woman Jesus spoke with was a Samaritan. In the eyes of the Jews, the Samaritans were a mixed race and should be avoided. She was also a known sinner and although women typically came in the morning and evening to draw water, she was there at about noon.[3]

What would you identify as this woman's disordered desires?

How do you think she felt as her personal life was laid bare?

What real desires did Jesus address for her?

Hope's Story

Hope confessed a tendency to hopscotch from one guy to another. She carried around an empty place she believed only a man could fill. Chasing down each new candidate for satisfaction was a lifestyle even if it meant surrendering pieces of her identity. Still, she found that once she caught the guy, he didn't complete her, and the vicious circle continued as she diverted her energy toward catching the next guy who might make her feel whole inside. Hope wanted to break the cycle and rely on Jesus to fill the desolate places. She made a start by acknowledging truth and asking Jesus to make it real in her heart.

My Disordered Craving

Sometimes the loudest and most deceptive desire of my heart is control. My trust in others was broken dramatically early on in life. The thought of being left again is scary. I fear being alone, so I work to control my surroundings and others' opinions of me. I desire to make everything okay all the time so I'll never need to fear abandonment again. But I am learning that my desire is misplaced. When I choose to seek Jesus, He meets my need for unconditional love; I am bathed in a knowing that He will never leave or forsake me (see Hebrews 13:5) and that nothing can separate me from His love (see Romans 8:38-39).

Describe any way in which you identify with either of the above-mentioned stories.

Read Isaiah 58:11. What would you identify as the parched ground of your life?

Luke 1:53 says, "He has filled the hungry with good things but has sent the rich away empty." Jesus is never brusque or uncaring when we come to Him hungry. His heart is welcoming, responsive, and tender to those who admit their need. If you are starving for wholeness, if you feel as though your heart resembles shards of broken glass or a war zone, the violence can end. Jesus is able to take you on a healing journey characterized more and more by wholehearted living.

Pause and take a desire inventory. List everything that pops into your mind. Lay your fears and longings before the Lord. Ask Him to pinpoint and shape your deepest yearnings, and jot down any thoughts that come to your mind.

Read Psalm 42:1-2 and Psalm 84 aloud, granting your heart permission to enter into the cry of the psalmist. Which phrases stand out to you?

Go back and read any verses that grab your heart, making them your prayer.

Abundance

Our hearts might be slow to learn sometimes, but living in the lavish abundance of relationship with Jesus can be surprising and delightful. At first we grab on as if to a mist but then find He's solid, substantial, and real. In John 10:10, Jesus said, "The thief comes only to steal and kill and destroy; I have come that they may have life, and have it to the full."

Let's read that verse in the *Amplified Bible* together:

The thief comes only in order to steal and kill and destroy. I came that they may have and enjoy life, and have it in abundance (to the full, till it overflows).

Now try placing your name in that verse. Voice it aloud as if Jesus were physically in the room right now speaking to you.

The thief comes only in order to steal, kill, and destroy. I came that _____ may have and enjoy life, and that _____ may have it in abundance (to the full, till it overflows).

Repeat this truth over and over until it begins to be more than just words.

Read Isaiah 55:1-3 below and underline any action words. Then circle phrases that are a result of taking those actions.

> Come, all you who are thirsty,
>> come to the waters;
> and you who have no money,
>> come, buy and eat!
> Come, buy wine and milk
>> without money and without cost.
> Why spend money on what is not bread,
>> and your labor on what does not satisfy?
> Listen, listen to me, and eat what is good,
>> and your soul will delight in the richest of fare.
> Give ear and come to me;
>> hear me, that your soul may live.
> I will make an everlasting covenant with you,
>> my faithful love promised to David.

Abundance, richness, and life are stamped all over this passage. Come to the table and indulge. The Lord has set a delectable life feast before us. Psalm 119:103 describes the sweetness: "How sweet are your words to my taste, sweeter than honey to my mouth!" I recently heard of a professor who placed a sheet of waxed paper over his students' Bibles. Then he dribbled a drop of honey on the waxed paper. The students were instructed to lift their Bibles to their mouths and taste the honey. Though I can't physically place honey on your Bibles, I hope you will dip your spirit in the sweetness of Jesus, that you will enjoy the feast He has set before you.

Please read the following verses from the book of Psalms:

> You prepare a table before me
>> in the presence of my enemies. (23:5)

They feast on the abundance of your house;
>   you give them drink from your river of delights. (36:8)

Imagine the Lord seating you at a beautifully set table. The ambiance is perfect, the lighting just right, and the place setting exquisite. A small sampler of the life feast is set before you. Take your time as you chew on each morsel. Taste every bite and record the details in the following table.

Scripture	This Bite Contains . . .
Psalm 103:1-4	
Isaiah 58:11	
Matthew 5:6	
John 4:14	
John 6:35,48-51	
John 15:11	
Ephesians 3:19	
Ephesians 5:18	
Philippians 4:12-13,19	
1 Timothy 1:14	

Which bites did you find most satisfying?

What about them appeals to you?

Sit quietly with Jesus, thanking Him for the feast. Say the name of Jesus. Let it linger on your lips. Bernard of Clairvaux wrote,

> The name of Jesus is also nourishment. Haven't you felt stronger when you think of it? There is no other name that can similarly bless the one who meditates on it. It has the ability to refresh and strengthen. The best intellectual food is dry until it is dipped in this oil.[4]

Meditate on the richness of Jesus' name. Worship the Lord by reading Psalm 63:1-8 from *The Message*:

God—you're my God!
     I can't get enough of you!
I've worked up such hunger and thirst for God,
     traveling across dry and weary deserts.

So here I am in the place of worship, eyes open,
     drinking in your strength and glory.
In your generous love I am really living at last!
     My lips brim praises like fountains.

I bless you every time I take a breath;
    My arms wave like banners of praise to you.

I eat my fill of prime rib and gravy;
    I smack my lips. It's time to shout praises!
If I'm sleepless at midnight,
    I spend the hours in grateful reflection.
Because you've always stood up for me,
    I'm free to run and play.
I hold on to you for dear life,
    And you hold me steady as a post.

How surprising it is to be full and satisfied yet still yearning for the ultimate feast. One day there will be a banquet unlike any we've ever attended. Please read Revelation 19:7-9. Give your imagination free rein for a few moments to fantasize about being at that wedding supper, seeing the Lord, bowing at His feet, and knowing a satisfaction beyond your grandest hopes and dreams. What whets your appetite for this day? What longing or anticipation does this passage create for you?

We can dream of the feast to come and live right now crying out, "God—you're my God! I can't get enough of you!"

A Picture of Satisfaction
Jesus is our source and our example. Though He knew He was headed for great pain, though He was rejected by His own people, Jesus had a satisfied heart. His personal fulfillment was not at the beck and call of public opinion or circumstances.

Read John 4:34 and John 17:1-5 and jot down any thoughts you have about these passages.

Jesus desired to bring the Father glory, to do His will, and that desire was wholly fulfilled. What would it look like for us to live with that desire trumping all others?

It seems counterintuitive that a satisfied spirit can be unearthed as we pour ourselves out for the glory of another. Yet when our desires coincide with the delight of knowing the Lord and making Him known, we find unmatched fulfillment.

Read the following passages:

Delight yourself in the LORD
    and he will give you the desires of your heart. (Psalm 37:4)

Your name and renown
    are the desire of our hearts. (Isaiah 26:8)

We, who with unveiled faces all reflect the Lord's glory, are being transformed into his likeness with ever-increasing glory, which comes from the Lord, who is the Spirit. (2 Corinthians 3:18)

What do you think is most likely to veil the glory of the Lord in your life?

How does digging into the life feast spread before us glorify God?

In what way might Jesus be inviting you to press into the desire to be so transformed that the glory of God is unveiled?

Reflect

If you are starving and can find nothing to satisfy your hunger, then come. Come, and you will be filled.

— JEANNE GUYON, *EXPERIENCING THE DEPTHS OF*
JESUS CHRIST

Please revisit Isaiah 55:1-3 and envision it as a personal invitation. Who is doing the inviting?

What are you invited to? Where? When?

Is there any cost? Is there anything you need to bring? Are there any specific directions?

Using a sheet of paper, a card, or an actual invitation, form this passage into a personal invitation. Place your invitation in an envelope addressed to your home, and then drop the invitation in the mail. When you receive it in the mail, take in all the details and go to the Lord and RSVP. Then describe your RSVP time in your journal.

If you have time, consider repeating the process with Matthew 11:28, Revelation 22:17, or another passage of your choosing.

Respond

Deuteronomy 8:10 exhorts, "When you have eaten and are satisfied, praise the LORD your God for the good land he has given you." Think back over the week. What have you eaten from the hand of Jesus?

What tastes, textures, and scents surprised or delighted you?

What desires are still yearning to be fulfilled?

How will you submit them to Jesus that He may form and fulfill them?

Brennan Manning reminded us that "the deepest desire of our hearts is for union with God."[5] The amazing truth is that Jesus brings that desire to fruition and carries nourishment to every corner of our hearts. How should we respond to His abundance? Nothing seems quite adequate. It seems the best we can do is turn into the abundance with open hands, receive it with gratitude, and live fully for His glory.

Revisit Psalm 63 and use it as an outline for offering your petition, thanksgiving, and praise to the Lord. Look to Him to provide a feast that unites your deepest desires with abundance.

Will you pray with me and continue as you feel led?

> *Lord Jesus, I hunger to know I am completely loved.*
> *I long for meaning and life. Sometimes relationships*
> *and daily life leave my heart empty, aching, and*
> *lonely. How I need to rest in Your presence. Draw*
> *me to Yourself, Jesus. You are life. You are love. You*
> *are more than worthy of all glory and praise. You fill*
> *my heart in ways I never thought possible. Pull me*
> *in close and satisfy my heart as only You can.*

Hold On Tight

In the classic story *Little Women*, Amy falls through the ice and needs rescuing. At first Jo stands immobilized, stunned by terror. Then she and Laurie together rescue Amy with the help of a hockey stick and fence rail.[1]

I, too, have stood by gaping helplessly as a fight for survival played out before me. A swimmer panicked and became disoriented, prompting a well-meaning bystander to jump into the water and save the floundering swimmer. Ultimately, the rescue was successful, but the franticness of the moment left a mark on me.

Lifeguards are warned about the urge to panic that many people experience when faced with imminent drowning. Lifeguards are instructed to approach the struggling person from the rear so he or she cannot pull the lifeguard under in panic. Then, if possible, the person hangs on to one side of a flotation device as the rescuer grabs the opposite side.[2] The goal is for the swimmer to be calmed enough to both grab hold and relax even though those actions seem contradictory.

When, if ever, have you battled the instinct to resort to disorienting panic?

In our spiritual walks, we have parallel instructions for surviving and thriving when all is well and when we're in the throes of threatening moments. We are to both hold on tight to the Lord and rest in Him. At first glance, those instructions seem divisive, but they actually reflect wholeness. Still, wild flailing sometimes comes far more naturally than a calm grip on the Lord. A recent song implores, "Please don't fight the hands that are holding you."[3] Imagine Jesus speaking those words directly to you. What emotion do you hear in His voice?

What is your gut-level response?

Please pray along with me:

> *Lord, I don't want to fight You. By Your grace, give me the ability to cling to You with all that I am.*

*Strengthen my grip; strengthen my spirit that I may
hold on to You ferociously and with surrender. I
say with the psalmist, "My flesh and my heart may
fail, but God [You are] the strength of my heart and
my portion forever" (Psalm 73:26). May my life
reflect this as I hold on and rest in Your strong arms.
Amen.*

Ponder Scripture

Please read Deuteronomy 30:19-20. The original Hebrew word translated "hold fast" is *qbd* or *dabaq*. It carries the meaning "to cling, stick, stay close, cleave, keep close, stick to, stick with, follow closely."[4]

Do any of the following phrases offer depth and texture to the Deuteronomy verse for you or resonate at this time in your life?

- Cling to Him
- Stick to Him
- Stay close to Him
- Cleave to Him
- Keep close to Him
- Stick with Him
- Follow closely to Him

The same word that exhorts us to "hold fast" in Deuteronomy is used in Psalm 63:8, which says, "My soul clings to you; your right hand upholds me." How does it feel to realize that while you are hanging on, even if by your fingertips, the Lord is upholding you?

A Hands-On Approach

My Story

Moving across the country to a completely unfamiliar area threatened daily to dislodge my grip. Upheaval became the norm. Our home in Colorado still hadn't sold, so I was living out of a suitcase in a motel room. Our new puppy, Lucy, was my constant companion while my husband traveled frequently for business. I needed a map to navigate my new surroundings, and those who know me well know I'm definitely directionally challenged. I fought a desperate sense of disconnection and loneliness. Over and over, the Lord reminded me that I was not in outer Mongolia, that I could not go anywhere where He was not already, and that I could do more than survive if I held on to Him for dear life. He already had a firm grip on me.

Cassie's Story

Cassie relayed her tendency to be thrown into a panic at the thought of being without the security of male companionship. She considered taking steps to reverse any signs of aging out of fear of losing her grip on the male species. The Lord dealt with her gently. One by one, he pried each finger loose and attached them to Him. She found freedom to make the most of her looks without the desperation attached.

Jennie's Story

Jennie clung to the pursuit of perfection. The idea that she must somehow become good enough for God to really love her had a death grip on her life. Defeat, weariness, and hopelessness followed her every day. Jesus pursued her steadfastly, luring her into His arms through countless avenues of truth. His Word gripped her heart, announcing news worth clinging to:

> He took our sin-dead lives and made us alive in Christ.
> He did all this on his own, with no help from us! Then he

picked us up and set us down in highest heaven in company with Jesus, our Messiah.

Now God has us where he wants us, with all the time in this world and the next to shower grace and kindness upon us in Christ Jesus. Saving is all his idea, and all his work. All we do is trust him enough to let him do it. It's God's gift from start to finish! (Ephesians 2:5-8, MSG)

In what way, if any, do you identify with the three stories?

When are you most likely to hold on to Jesus for dear life?

Faithful Flailing

Before reading the following passages in Matthew and Mark, it's helpful to be aware of some background information. "The Jews (as well as the Romans) usually divided the night into four watches, of three hours each. The first watch began at six, the second at nine, the third at twelve, and the fourth at three in the morning."[5] Also, keep in the back of your mind that the disciples had just witnessed Jesus feeding five thousand men, plus women and children. Then Jesus made the disciples get in a boat and go on ahead of Him.

Please read Matthew 14:22-33 and Mark 6:47-52, keeping your

eyes open for details. Read through the Matthew passage again, this time aloud. As you read, let your eyes adjust to the dark and feel the wind and the spray of the water as you are whipped around. Inhale and smell the scent of the storm. Imagine what would happen in the pit of your stomach when you saw a figure walking across the water. Feel the terror and hear the disciples' cries.

Try drawing a graph tracing the disciples' emotions from the time Jesus told them to get in the boat until He joined them and they worshipped him.

Next draw a graph depicting Peter's emotions.

The immediate response of Jesus in Matthew 14:27 is comforting. Have you personally experienced Jesus' calming presence in the midst of fear? If so, describe that time.

The Message translates verse 28 as "Peter, suddenly bold, said, 'Master, if it's really you, call me to come to you on the water.'" Journal about a time you felt "suddenly bold" and then freaked out when you realized the magnitude of your action.

Peter goes forward clinging to what he's seen of Jesus up to this point. When he does falter, Jesus is instantly there to reach out and catch him. There are probably many ways Jesus could have rescued Peter from the waves, but "he reached down and grabbed his hand" (verse 31, MSG).

Pretend you are Peter. What's going through your mind as Jesus takes hold of you?

How would you feel after a skin-to-skin rescue?

- ◆ Fearful
- ◆ Comforted
- ◆ Cherished
- ◆ Safe
- ◆ Unaffected
- ◆ Other _____

Read through Matthew 14:22-33 one more time and sit silently for a few minutes. Record in your journal any additional thoughts.

A Personal Storm

This summer a storm swirled around me as my husband faced a serious diagnosis and dangerous surgeries. He was hospitalized in a city where I knew no one. I spent many lonely nights in a hotel room feeling an unnamed dread in the pit of my stomach. I watched helplessly as pain engulfed him and nearly stole his life. The future seemed covered in volatile, scary clouds. Peter's words "Lord, save me!" could have been mine.

But in those moments of my greatest need, Jesus' whisper became almost tangible. He reminded me, "Rita, you know Me." I clung to the truth of His love demonstrated on the Cross, His active presence throughout my life, His character. Still, I often felt ripped apart by the idea that only a miraculous healing could fit my faith. I needed some reassurance our physical future would be whole. It was in those moments that Jesus calmed the wind and waves again and again saying, "Rita, be still and know I am God. It is enough that I hold the future."

Try reading the following phrase from Psalm 46:10 aloud, emphasizing a different word each time:

Be still, and know that I am God.
Be **still**, and know that I am God.
Be still, and **know** that I am God.
Be still, and know that **I am God.**

Which of these words most touches your heart today?

Describe an occasion when Jesus met you or someone you know in a time of desperation or fear of the future.

Max Lucado said, "Meet today's problems with today's strength. Don't start tackling tomorrow's problems until tomorrow. You do not have tomorrow's strength yet. You simply have enough for today."[6] What strength has Jesus supplied you for today?

Settling Touch

Lucy, my new Schipperke puppy, and I attended dog training, and I learned a new command: "Settle." In times when Lucy became over-excited, fearful, or just plain wild and unable to calm herself, I had a new technique to help her settle down. Placing one hand firmly on her belly and the other around her body, I simply held her until she stopped wriggling. Eventually she exhaled, I felt her muscles relax, and she rested in my arms.

At times when we are so worked up we can't seem to "settle," we need a touch from Jesus. The wonderful thing is Jesus isn't reticent about touching, holding, or carrying His beloved. He doesn't draw back if we're in pain, leprous, contagious, nervous, consumed with busyness, or afraid.

Read Psalm 18:16; Isaiah 40:11; Matthew 8:3,15; 17:7; Mark 10:16; Luke 13:10-13; 15:4-6; and John 10:28. Note the physical love of Jesus. Which of these verses captures your attention and why?

What kind of touch settles your heart?

There are beautiful children's books for infants and toddlers that provide a sensory experience. For example, a book about baby animals includes a textured area to touch as the caption is read. If you were putting together a brief sensory book on the textures of Jesus' touch, what would you include?

Reflect

If I rise on the wings of the dawn,
   if I settle on the far side of the sea,
even there your hand will guide me,
   your right hand will hold me fast.

— PSALM 139:9-10

How comforting to know that Jesus holds us fast, but are there ways we resist? Sometimes I know I am not fully cooperative; I dangle out there grabbing whatever I think looks secure at the moment instead of turning into His arms. As I was sharing with my friend this desire to turn into Jesus' grasp, she immediately was reminded of her ballroom dancing lessons and a move called "the cuddle." Needing a visual, I turned to the Internet and was surprised to find that this move is known in many forms of dancing.

If, like me, you need to see a demonstration, search for "dance move the cuddle" and choose the type of dance you want to watch. Whether or not you see a visual, consider exploring one of the following reflection exercises as you reverently turn into Jesus' arms:

- Choreograph a worship song such as "Draw Me Close." With each movement—the dips, twirls, footwork, cuddle—lean into Jesus. Imagine holding and being held, moving toward and away from, and try to give physical expression to the song. If you like, play the song and have a private dance with Jesus. Journal any thoughts, feelings, or impressions you have.
- Sway quietly in your seat as you play or hum your favorite worship song. Open and close your hands. Imagine holding on to Jesus and Him holding on to you. Lean into the moment and be still for a few minutes. Then journal any thoughts, feelings, or impressions you have.

Respond

Calvin Miller wrote of the connecting power of hand-holding throughout his relationship with his wife:

This simple act has kept our union safe.
Anything can happen, when you forget to practice the art.
You can slip, or lose your way, or be run down.
We have practiced the art until we have refined it.
We never cross a busy street without the counsel of this
clasp,

'cause in the uncertainties of this life, you just never
know.[7]

How does holding on to Jesus affect your union with Him?

How can you practice the art of hand-holding with Jesus throughout
the good and challenging moments of this week? Try to be specific and
then be intentional.

Stretch out your hands to the Lord and imagine that His touch sur-
rounds you as you close this week's study with the following prayer:

Be Christ this day my strong protector:
Against poison and burning,
Against drowning and wounding,
Through reward wide and plenty . . .
Christ beside me, Christ before me;
Christ behind me, Christ within me;
Christ beneath me, Christ above me;
Christ to right of me, Christ to left of me;
Christ in my lying, my sitting, my rising;
Christ of all who know me,
Christ on tongue of all who meet me,
Christ in eye of all who see me,
Christ in ear of all who hear me.[8]

Living as Beloved

Marriage proposals have become diverse over the years. Some suitors light up the scoreboards at sporting events with "Marry me, Mandy," while others write it out on white sandy beaches. Not long ago, I had the privilege of knowing a romantic secret. A friend was preparing to propose to his girlfriend as a few other women and I drooled over the moment to come. He knew the caretaker of a particular park that boasted a beautiful gazebo near a lit fountain. He asked his girlfriend to meet him in the park and planned for the caretaker to flip a switch at just the right moment, lighting up the fountain and his proposal. Each detail fell neatly into place, he popped the big question on bended knee, and she said, "Yes!" Their engagement officially began.

Engagements are all about promise, the promise of exclusivity, lasting love, and building a joint future. Today, however, an engagement can mean going to the next level and might or might not be taken as a seriously binding commitment. Years ago, Jewish people called the step just prior to marriage "betrothal."

> Betrothal with the Jews was a serious matter, not lightly entered into and not lightly broken. The man who betrothed a maiden was legally husband ... and "an informal

cancelling of betrothal was impossible." Though they did not live together as husband and wife till actual marriage, breach of faithfulness on the part of the betrothed was treated as adultery.[1]

As believers, we are the beloved bride of Christ; we are betrothed to the Lord Jesus. How reassuring to know He doesn't take His commitment to us lightly. How do you feel about being betrothed to Jesus as you await the final wedding supper of the Lamb?

Ponder Scripture

In Song of Songs 5:9, the friends ask, "How is your beloved better than others, most beautiful of women?" If friends were to ask us this question about Jesus, what could we say? We could begin with the titles given Him in Scripture, such as:

- ♦ Wonderful Counselor
- ♦ Mighty God
- ♦ Everlasting Father
- ♦ Prince of Peace
- ♦ Messiah
- ♦ King of kings and Lord of lords
- ♦ Redeemer
- ♦ Lion of Judah
- ♦ Lamb of God
- ♦ The Good Shepherd
- ♦ Savior

The Lover of our souls, the one we are betrothed to, is all of this and more. And it is this same Jesus who proclaims eternal love for us in John 15:9, saying, "As the Father has loved me, so have I loved you. Now remain in my love."

Please read Matthew 3:17 and 17:5, Luke 9:35, and 2 Peter 1:17, noting the love of the Father for Jesus. Try to picture that kind of love. How does the Father refer to Jesus?

Julian of Norwich wrote in *Revelations of Divine Love,*

> We are so preciously loved by God that we cannot even comprehend it. No created being can ever know how much and how sweetly and tenderly God loves them. It is only with the help of his grace that we are able to persevere in spiritual contemplation with endless wonder at his high, surpassing, immeasurable love which our Lord in his goodness has for us.[2]

The extravagant love of the Father for Jesus goes beyond what words describe, yet it's the same love that Jesus lavishes on us. We are His, the beloved of the Lord Jesus Christ, and He exhorts us to remain (abide, dwell, make our home in) His love. Go back to John 15:9 and read it again. Brainstorm ways you could practically revel in, soak in, or live in the amazing truth of this verse. Pick one possibility and commit to trying it out in the coming week.

Marked as His Beloved

In Song of Songs 2:4, it says, "His banner over me is love." This is a figurative banner, but in the Old Testament, tribes were sometimes marked by an actual banner.[3] How does it feel to be marked by the love of Jesus?

Try on the sound of the following truth of the banner marking you as His:

I am [insert your name], the beloved of Jesus.

We love the ring of that phrase, but sometimes other titles, other banners, encroach on our living space, isolating pieces of our hearts. Banners like:

- I am _____the alone.
- I am_____the timid.
- I am_____the worthless.
- I am_____the unlovable.
- I am_____the fearful.

Are any phrases like these crowding out truth and dividing your heart? If so, name them and show them to Jesus. Hold them up to the light of John 15:9. Ask Jesus to take over and unite your heart under the banner of knowing that you are His beloved.

Consider praying this prayer based on words from Ephesians 3:18-19 (MSG):

> *Lord, plant both my feet firmly on love, help me*
> *to take in with all your followers the extravagant*
> *dimensions of Your love. Help me reach out and*
> *experience the breadth! Test its length! Plumb the*

depths! Rise to the heights! Lord, I want to live a full life in You. Amen.

Henri Nouwen wrote,

Every time you listen with great attentiveness to the voice that calls you the Beloved, you will discover within yourself a desire to hear that voice longer and more deeply. It is like discovering a well in the desert. Once you've touched wet ground, you want to dig deeper.[4]

Return once again to listening to this truth: "I am [your name], Jesus' beloved." Whisper it. Repeat it over and over. Shout it in delight from the rooftops. Journal about any ways you can make it your practice to increasingly listen to the voice of the Lord calling you His beloved.

Optional Exercise

Design or print out a banner (computer-generated, poster board, or other material) that proclaims in bold letters, "I am [insert your name], Jesus' beloved." Make it as large or small as fits your specific environment. Then hang it in a place of honor for the week.

A Receptive Life

Just yesterday I witnessed a conversation we've probably all heard at one time or another. Perhaps we've even participated in one just like it. A woman complimented her friend's jacket and the response was, "Oh, this? These are my fat clothes." The woman quickly admonished her friend, saying, "Come on, that was a compliment. Just accept it and say, 'Thank you.'" It's so hard sometimes to simply receive a compliment and say "thank you." As the beloved, we are not required to earn life.

Is there any sense in which Jesus is calling you "beloved" and you resist or diminish His words?

What would it look like to gratefully embrace His banner of love as a gift?

Please read Colossians 2:6-8. Verse 6 says that we live in Jesus just as we received Him. That's a slippery concept to nail down. When you received Jesus, how did you feel?

- ◆ Amazed by grace
- ◆ Stilled and at peace
- ◆ Full of gratitude
- ◆ Full of delight
- ◆ Full of wonder
- ◆ Invited
- ◆ Other _____

What does it mean to you to receive ongoing life in Jesus?

Continue reading Colossians 2:6-10. "Hollow" and "deceptive" aptly characterize the lesser identities I sometimes dabble in or places I go looking for life. Philosophies of this world have definitely infiltrated my thinking, especially as they regard achievement or performance. There are times I've given everything I had, hoping for applause, but as soon as the applause died down, I was still empty. As Henri Nouwen said, "The world and its strategies may help you to survive for a long time, but they cannot help you live because the world is not the source even of its own life, let alone yours."[5]

Some women tell me they've bought into the deceptive idea that their worth is based on looks, getting to or staying a size 2, keeping all wrinkles camouflaged, or trying to look the part of superwoman. They say there's no real satisfaction in that pursuit even if they somehow attain a model look. Loitering in the background of their hearts is the truth that who they are goes so much further than skin-deep, and the acceptance feels tenuous and unreal.

What hollow or deceptive ideas threaten your heart with captivity?

Read Colossians 2:10 again, noting what is given to those who are Christ's beloved. In *The Message*, verse 10 is worded like this:

> Everything of God gets expressed in him, so you can see and hear him clearly. You don't need a telescope, a microscope, or a horoscope to realize the fullness of Christ, and the emptiness of the universe without him. When you come to him, that fullness comes together for you, too. His power extends over everything.

Jesus is the ultimate authority on how He sees you and who He's created you to be, and He calls you "beloved." His view of you trumps all others. Are you beginning to lean into that truth? If so, how does it shape your self-talk?

How does it shape your interaction with others?

Life is a gift and living it out is also a gift, each day pulling up lies and becoming more rooted in truth, resting in our place as the beloved. Using Psalm 86 as a guide, ask the Lord to deal with the hollow and deceptive philosophies that threaten you. Pour out your desire for an undivided heart that rests in His love.

A Transformational Root System

In a scene in the movie *Nights in Rodanthe*, Adrienne, played by Diane Lane, is grieving the death of the man she loves. As she talks with her daughter about him, she raves about having a love that makes you the best you can be and urges you to become more. She implores her daughter to never settle for less than a transforming love. Her daughter sees the impact of that love in her mom's life and nods as comprehension registers in her eyes.

Imagine that like Adrienne's daughter, those around us begin to notice the beauty. They start to toy with the possibility that something amazing like becoming the beloved is possible. Revelation 22:17 calls out, "The Spirit and the bride say, 'Come!' And let him who hears say, 'Come!' Whoever is thirsty, let him come; and whoever wishes, let him take the free gift of the water of life." Our lives can be multi-dimensional invitations to know Jesus. We say, "Come," by living as beloved. We are grafted into Jesus' holy invitation to know Him; to be saved; to hear His voice and see His face; to live cherished, freed, and satisfied. It's our honor as the betrothed, as the bride, to become so breathtaking it's visible.

Have you ever met someone whose life invited you to abundant life? What was refreshing about that person's life?

What is Jesus doing in your life today to sculpt a breathtaking life that invites others to know Him?

Reflect

I am certain of this one thing: Jesus loves me, I can make it! I have found his love steadfast in every venture. I have claimed "Jesus loves me" as my musical testament. I rarely sing aloud, but for sixty years now its enabling melody has ricocheted through the corridors of my heart. No trial has silenced the

*song. No tempest has dulled the tune. Jesus loves me, I can
make it. His love is my mode of survival, my liberation from
myself, my way of triumph.*
— CALVIN MILLER, *JESUS LOVES ME*

What can you passionately proclaim to be true about Jesus' love for
you?

Song of Songs 6:3 says, "I am my lover's and my lover is mine."
Jesus is the lover of your soul and you belong to Him. You're betrothed
to Him, destined to consummate that marriage for all eternity.

Human weddings celebrate love and are meant to reveal the shape
of the union between Christ and His people. Think about the wedding
vows couples make. They say things like "to have and to hold from this
day forward, forsaking all others and clinging only unto him." Couples
make vows to love and cherish till death parts them. But there's no
parting ahead for you and Jesus—just the opposite. There's a heart-
stopping moment of meeting yet to come.

Imagine that moment when you will gaze directly into the eyes of
the holy and awesome Lover of your soul. If you are even able to speak,
what might you say?

Until that amazing day comes, we can ask for grace to live life as a promise. Experiment with writing out some vows to speak aloud today to Jesus and what He might say to you, His beloved (based on what you know of Him from Scripture).

Respond

Please turn to John 12:1-3. As you read, see the scene play out in your mind. Watch Mary's love become costly and extravagant.

Now turn for a moment to Luke 10:38-42 and John 11:29-44 and read some of the transforming moments of Mary's journey, moments spent at the feet of Jesus. Reflect on where Mary has been. She has endured misunderstanding and criticism from family because of her passion for Jesus. She became intimate with crushing grief, disappointment, and "Why, God?" questions. She saw her brother miraculously resurrected. He was at this dinner in the John 12 passage. What must she have felt every time she looked at Lazarus and then at Jesus? Because of knowing Jesus, her life would never be the same, and that relationship with Him freed her to pour out her heart holding nothing in reserve. She laid it all out at His feet.

Think back over your journey with Jesus. When have you found yourself at Jesus' feet?

When have you known Him in a way that demands wholehearted adoration?

Have there been times when it seemed your heart was turned inside out by loss?

Choose a few of those moments and try to construct a graph of momentous highs and lows in your journey with the Lord. Where are you right now?

In light of where you've been, your present, and the knowledge that nothing can ever separate you from the love of Jesus (see Romans 8:37-39), will you bow down and worship?

If you are able, physically kneel at the feet of Jesus, let His love suffuse your entire being, and respond to that love in worship.

Conclude your time with the following prayer, written by Elizabeth Basset:

 My God, I desire to love thee perfectly,

With all my heart which thou madest for thyself
With all my mind, which only thou canst satisfy

With all my soul, which feign would soar to thee.
With all my strength, my feeble strength, which shrinks before
So great a task and yet can choose naught else but spend itself
In loving thee.

Claim thou my heart,
Fill thou my mind,
Uplift my soul and
Reinforce my strength,
That when I failthou mayest succeed in me
And make me love thee perfectly.[6]

Review

1. After these past eight weeks of this Bible study, how has your heart gained any wholeness?
2. In weeks 1 through 4, which scriptures had the deepest impact on your heart?
3. In weeks 5 through 8, which scriptures had the deepest impact on your heart?
4. As you view your relationship with Jesus as the ultimate love story, what places in your heart need the most tender loving care right now?
5. How could you apply Scripture as a healing and unifying comfort?

Notes

Week 1: To Know Him Is to Love Him
1. Charles F. Weigle, "No One Ever Cared for Me Like Jesus," 1932.
2. John of the Cross, quoted in Brent Curtis and John Eldredge, *The Sacred Romance: Drawing Closer to the Heart of God* (Nashville: Thomas Nelson, 1997), 97.
3. Calvin Miller, *Celtic Devotions* (Downers Grove, IL: InterVarsity, 2008), 115–116.

Week 2: Complete Freedom
1. "Holding Out for a Hero" by Jim Steinman and Dean Pitchford, performed by Bonnie Tyler, *Footloose* soundtrack, © 1984.
2. I. Howard Marshall, A. R. Millard, J. I. Packer, and D. J. Wiseman, eds., *New Bible Dictionary*, 3rd ed. (Downers Grove, IL: InterVarsity, 1996), 451.
3. Cynthia Spell Humbert, *Deceived by Shame, Desired by God* (Colorado Springs, CO: NavPress, 2001), 21.
4. Dr. Bruce Demarest, *Soul Guide: Following Jesus as Spiritual Director* (Colorado Springs, CO: NavPress, 2003), 88.
5. Humbert, 49.
6. Demarest, 89.
7. Henri Nouwen, quoted in Demarest, 88.

Week 3: Shaped by Perfect Love
1. Margery Williams, *The Velveteen Rabbit* (New York: Avon Books, 1975), 12–13.
2. Simon Tugwell, quoted in Brennan Manning, *Abba's Child: The Cry of the Heart for Intimate Belonging* (Colorado Springs, CO: NavPress, 1994), 18.

3. David G. Benner, *The Gift of Being Yourself: The Sacred Call to Self-Discovery* (Downers Grove, IL: InterVarsity, 2004), 92.

4. "Clay and Water" by Margaret Becker, *Falling Forward*, © 1998 Sparrow Records.

5. C. S. Lewis, quoted in John Ortberg, *The Life You've Always Wanted: Spiritual Disciplines for Ordinary People* (Grand Rapids, MI: Zondervan, 2002), 164.

6. Henri J. M. Nouwen, *Reaching Out: The Three Movements of the Spiritual Life* (New York: Image Books/Doubleday, 1975), 25.

7. Sandra Wilson, quoted in Siang-Yang Tan, *Rest: Experiencing God's Peace in a Restless World* (Vancouver: Regent College Publishing, 2000), 209.

8. Dennis Linn, Sheila Fabricant Linn, and Matthew Linn, *Sleeping with Bread: Holding What Gives You Life* (Mahaw, NY: Paulist Press, 1995), 1.

Week 4: Awake to His Voice

1. Jan Harris, *Quiet in His Presence: Experiencing God's Love Through Silent Prayer* (Grand Rapids, MI: Baker Books, 2003), 31.

2. Dallas Willard, *The Spirit of the Disciplines: Understanding How God Changes Lives* (New York: HarperCollins, 1988), 163.

3. Willard, 163–164.

Week 5: Adoring Gaze

1. James Strong, LLD, STD, *The New Strong's Expanded Dictionary of Bible Words* (Nashville: Thomas Nelson, 2001), 1079.

2. Spiros Zodhiates, ThD, ed., *The Complete Wordstudy Dictionary: New Testament* (Chattanooga, TN: AMG Publishers, 1992), 573.

3. C. S. Lewis, quoted in Howard Baker, *The One True Thing: What Is Worthy of Your Lifelong Devotion?* (Colorado Springs, CO: NavPress, 2007), 32.

4. I. Howard Marshall, A. R. Millard, J. I. Packer, and D. J. Wiseman, eds., *New Bible Dictionary*, 3rd ed. (Downers Grove,

IL: InterVarsity, 1996), 1077–1078.

5. Robertson's Word Pictures, www.searchgodsword.org/com/rwp/ view.cgi?book=lk&chapter=007&verse=036.

6. Harper Lee, quoted in Brennan Manning, *The Importance of Being Foolish: How to Think Like Jesus* (New York: HarperCollins, 2005), 41.

7. Mary Dorsett and Sharon Beougher, *Women and Evangelism: An Evangelistic Lifestyle from a Woman's Perspective* (Wheaton, IL: Billy Graham Center, Institute of Evangelism, 1994), 186.

8. Mother Teresa, quoted in Norman Shawchuck and Rueben P. Job, *A Guide to Prayer for All Who Seek God* (Nashville: Upper Room, 2003), 192.

9. Mother Teresa, quoted in Shawchuck and Job, 350.

10. John B. Dykes, "Jesus, the Very Thought of Thee," 1823–1876.

Week 6: Wholly Satisfied

1. *The American Heritage Dictionary* (Boston: Houghton Mifflin, 1985), s.v. "Satisfaction."

2. David G. Benner, *Desiring God's Will: Aligning Our Hearts with the Heart of God* (Downers Grove, IL: InterVarsity, 2005), 85–86.

3. *NIV Life Application Study Bible (New International Version)*, notes John 4:7-29.

4. Bernard of Clairvaux, quoted in *The Little Book of Hours: Praying with the Community of Jesus* (Brewster, MA: Paraclete Press, 2003), 98.

5. Brennan Manning, *Abba's Child: The Cry of the Heart for Intimate Belonging* (Colorado Springs, CO: NavPress, 1994), 38.

Week 7: Hold On Tight

1. Louisa May Alcott, *Little Women* (Wheaton, IL: Tyndale, 1997), 84.

2. How to Rescue Someone from Drowning, www.howcast.com/ guides/2131.

3. "By Your Side," by Tenth Avenue North. Copyright 2008, Franklin, TN: Reunion Records.

4. "hold fast," Old Testament Hebrew Lexicon, www .searchgodsword.org/lex/heb/view.cgi?number=12692.

5. Matthew 14, Wesley's Explanatory Notes, searchgodsword.org/ com/wen/view.cgi?book=mt&chapter=014&verse=031.

6. Max Lucado, quoted in Michael J. Wilkins, *The NIV Application Commentary, Matthew* (Grand Rapids, MI: Zondervan, 2004), 305.

7. Calvin Miller, *Life Is Mostly Edges* (Nashville: Thomas Nelson, 2008), 184.

8. "The Breastplate of St. Patrick," quoted in Calvin Miller, *Into the Depths of God: Where Eyes See the Invisible, Ears Hear the Inaudible, and Minds Conceive the Inconceivable* (Minneapolis: Bethany, 2000), 81.

Week 8: Living as Beloved

1. "betrothal," Robertson's Word Pictures of the New Testament, Matthew 1:18, www.searchgodsword.org/com/rwp/view.cgi?book =mt&chapter=001&verse=018.

2. Julian of Norwich, quoted in Richard J. Foster and James Bryan Smith, eds., *Devotional Classics: Selected Readings for Individuals and Groups* (New York: HarperCollins, 2005), 77.

3. I. Howard Marshall, A. R. Millard, J. I. Packer, and D.J. Wiseman, eds., *New Bible Dictionary*, 3rd ed. (Downers Grove, IL: InterVarsity, 1996), 119.

4. Henri J. M. Nouwen, *Life of the Beloved: Spiritual Living in a Secular World* (New York: Crossroad, 1992), 37.

5. Nouwen, 32.

6. Elizabeth Basset, "Love Is My Meaning," quoted in Rueben P. Job and Norman Shawchuck, *A Guide to Prayer for Ministers and Other Servants* (Nashville: Upper Room, 1983), 50.

About the Author

Rita Platt is a speaker, writer, and workshop leader who focuses on delighting in and experiencing deeper relationship with God. She is passionate about knowing the Lord with her head and her heart and inspiring others to walk in intimate relationship with Him. She is currently pursuing an MA in professional counseling with an emphasis on soul care. She is a certified Prepare/Enrich premarital and marital counselor. Rita holds a BA in communication, has a certificate in women and evangelism from the Billy Graham Center, and is a trained infant-adoption liaison. She also participated in an intensive week of training at the Leighton Ford Evangelism Leadership Conference.

Rita served for years as counseling coordinator at the Colorado Springs Pregnancy Center. She wrote materials for use in training and in the counseling room, including a brochure titled *Reflections for Your Journey*, used to introduce women to the Lord. The *Reflections* brochure was translated into Russian for use in some pregnancy centers in Russia. Rita has also served in church ministry as a child and family ministry director, initiating and creating new programs. She is a trained Parenting with Love and Logic facilitator and has authored articles titled "Silent Release" and "Advice for Parents of Prodigals." In addition, Rita served as worship leader for a single moms' ministry.

Rita, her husband, Thom, and Schipperke puppy, Lucy, recently relocated from Colorado Springs, Colorado, to Columbia, Maryland. Rita loves and is involved in music, performance art, and visual arts. Her hobbies include photographing waterfalls, knitting, and reading.

Other Bible studies from Rita Platt and more!

I Am His
Rita Platt

978-1-60006-387-9

Get to know your tender, wise, and powerful Abba Father. Through personal stories, creative interaction with Scripture, quiet reflection, and guided responses, the wonder of living as a child of God can come alive and be more accessible to a woman's heart. This eight-week study includes review and discussion questions.

Step into the Waters
Rita Platt

978-160006-389-3

Let your heart experience the abundant flow of living water and immerse yourself in life-giving intimacy with the Spirit. In *Step into the Waters*, women can connect deeply with the Holy Spirit through Scripture, personal stories, discussion questions, and spiritual disciplines. This eight-week study includes review and discussion questions.

The Amazing Collection
Big Dream Ministries, Inc.

THE AMAZING COLLECTION is a DVD Bible study taught book by book. The forty-five-minute DVDs with workbooks bring the main characters and the theme of each book of the Bible alive with dynamic teaching, original music videos, and personal testimonies.